SPORT PARACHUTING

by

RUSSELL A. GUNBY

Illustrated by

LEE SOPER

"Out of 10,000 feet of fall, always remember that the last half inch hurts the most. If you keep this in mind it will give you the necessary nonchalance for a successful jump."

—Captain Charles W. Purcell, 1932

The saving of two lives has been credited to memorized procedures taught in this book. It would appear, then, that its worth has been proven.

PUBLISHED BY R. A. GUNBY

1st Printing—1960
2d Printing—1961
3d Printing—1963
(Revised Edition)

LITHOGRAPHED BY HERALD PRINTERS & PUBLISHERS, MONTEREY, CALIFORNIA

TABLE OF CONTENTS

Introduction

PREFACE

This handbook originated because the recent wide acceptance and rapid growth of sport parachuting in the U.S. has created a serious need for standardization in the many techniques of this wonderful new sport. It is to the public, the curious newcomer to sport parachuting, and the new forming clubs that this book is dedicated so that parachute training and jumping may proceed along similar lines for all.

Herein you will find interesting historical events leading up to today's safe equipment, the descriptive terms used in the sport, and some idea about one's first parachute jump. Parachutes are described and shown in their major components. Techniques presently being used to exit from aircraft, control the body during delayed falls, manipulate the parachute, and landing are illustrated and explained for the newcomer.

Information has also been included for directors and organizers on parachuting rules, organization of clubs, a basic training program, and club forms and check lists. An outline for instructors on each period of training is also included as an aid to teacher and student alike.

The functional information in this book has been developed and proven in actual use. Systems and equipment described herein work. However, it should be remembered that there are other ways of doing the things described. Where one technique was known to be **safer** than another, particularly for students, then the **safest** one was selected to be shown.

Parachutes and parachuting techniques have been advancing for the past 500 years and, with the advent of the new sport of sky diving, will undoubtedly advance even more rapidly from now on.

Meanwhile, here is a **basic** guide for the public, the new parachutist, and the new club organizer.

For Safer Parachuting

R. A. GUNBY
Parachutist

4

PIONEERS IN PARACHUTING

Written history on parachuting is scarce and conflicting and many ideas and events have been lost; however, here are some of the basic facts about people and places that contributed toward today's wonderful new sport of sky diving.

DATE	EVENT
?	The umbrella was made by the Chinese. It is not impossible that some wise oriental looked up at his umbrella on a windy day and came up with some ideas about making and using a parachute!
1495 Italy	Leonarda da Vinci designed a parachute using a pyramid of cloth. It is known that da Vinci made models of his many inventions; however, no proof exists that he actually made any workable parachutes. As a point of interest, many of the features shown in da Vinci's early sketches are used in our parachutes of today!
1590 to 1690	During this time Galileo and Newton found that all falling bodies fall at the same rate of speed and that falling speed increases at a uniform rate until a constant speed, or terminal velocity, is reached.

Fig. 1, da Vinci's Parachute

1617 **Italy**	Fouste Veranzio jumped from a tower in Venice using a square, wooden framework covered with canvas as a parachute.
1783 **France**	The Montgolfier brothers, while performing experiments with hot air balloons, made and tested some different parachutes. In one experiment they dropped a sheep safely to the ground from a high tower using a seven foot parachute.
1783 **France**	Sebastian Leormand used a 14 foot parachute in jumping from a high tower in an endeavor to perfect a way of escaping safely from a burning building.
1785 **France**	J. P. Blanchard took a dog up in a balloon and successfully dropped the dog to the ground by parachute. Blanchard also performed other parachute experiments among which was designing a parachute made of silk which could be folded. Heretofore all other models were attached to some form of framework which held the cloth open. Doubt exists as to whether Blanchard ever actually jumped himself. Unofficially it was reported that he broke a leg during a parachute jump in 1793 and then gave up any further experiments.

Fig. 2, Blanchard's Parachute

1797
France
Credit for being the first parachutist generally goes to Andrew Jacques Garnerin who made so many experiments and demonstrations that, even though it was rumored Blanchard made a jump before this, Garnerin probably deserves the credit. On October 22, 1797, at Paris, Garnerin jumped into the basket of his parachute which was slung under a hot air balloon, was taken aloft to about 2000 feet, and cut loose. The parachute quickly opened and Garnerin came down safely and triumphantly. In 1802, near London, England, Garnerin, now a full time parachutist, used a new 23 foot, 32 silk panel parachute in a demonstration for English royalty. Again slung under a balloon, he is believed to have risen to about 8000 feet before being cut loose. His inverted, cup-shaped parachute again functioned properly and checked his fall; however, the 'chute oscillations were so violent all the way to the ground that he was badly shaken up and airsick from the ride. As a result of this jump, a French scientist solved the oscillation problem by suggesting that a hole be cut at the apex of the cup to permit the caught air to escape out of the top instead of unevenly at the skirt or sides.

Fig. 3, Garnerin's Parachute

6

1808 Poland	A Polish balloonist named Kuparento jumped from a burning balloon over Warsaw and became the first man to save his life by using an emergency parachute.
1837 England	On July 24th, 1837, Robert Cocking, (who had watched Garnerin's 1802 jump) after years of working on parachute designs to make them safer, decided to try out his perfected model. It was large and cone shaped with the cone apex pointing **downward**. The top connected to a 107 foot ring and smaller rings supported the lower sections. It used 124 yards of linen and was believed to have weighed over 200 pounds. When Cocking released the parachute from beneath the ascending balloon at 5000 feet, the parachute started a rapid, erring descent. The strain broke the 107 foot upper ring, the cloth ripped and collapsed, and at approximately 300 feet above the ground the basket fell off and carried Cocking to his death.

Fig. 4, Cocking's Parachute

1838 America	John Wise, a balloonist, twice permitted his balloon to explode at 13,000 feet. The under portion of the bag then inverted up under the top into an inverted cup shape and he descended safely.
1885 America	A collapsible silk parachute was introduced by Captain Thomas Baldwin.
1903 America	A powered aircraft, made by the Wright Brothers, made its first successful flight.
1910 Italy	An Italian inventor named Pino introduced a back packed parachute which had an attached aviators cap containing a small pilot chute, which, when activated, blossomed from the cap and pulled the large back packed parachute from the container. This pilot chute feature is still in use today.
1911 America	Grant Morton, carrying a folded silk parachute in his arms, jumped from a Wright Model B airplane over Venice Beach, California, and landed safely.
1911 Russia	A Russian inventor, G. E. Kotelnikov, had his experimental parachute designs rejected by the Russian Air Force because it was felt that pilots would be tempted to jump rather than save their aircraft.
1912 America	Capt. Albert Berry made a demonstration jump from a pusher type airplane using a parachute packed in a cone-shaped cylinder outside the fuselage over the wheel axle. He crawled down onto the axle, slid onto a trapeze bar, (which acted as his harness) shoved off at a height of about 2500 feet, and landed safely.

1917 **Europe**	With the advent of aerial warfare, a need for an efficient parachute was felt by all nations. As a result, the Germans adopted the Heinecke parachute, the British the Mears and the Guardian Angel, the French the Orrs and S.T.A., and the Americans the A.E.F. These parachutes were heavy and cumbersom, worked on the "static line" principle, were not safe in speeds over 100 mph, and most pilots regarded them with disdain.
1919 **America**	The US Army directed Major W. L. Hoffman and Mr. Floyd Smith to conduct research and experiments at McCook Field, Dayton, Ohio, to construct safe and foolproof parachutes, a project started by Mr. Smith the year before.
1919 **America**	On April 28th, Leslie L. Irvin conducted the first human test of a free fall parachute at McCook Field, Ohio. In a plane piloted by Floyd Smith, he jumped clear of the plane at 1500 feet, pulled the opening cord, and the chute immediately blossomed above him. Though Irvin broke his ankle on landing, through no fault of the parachute, the first test was a success.
1922 **America**	On October 22nd, Lieutenant Harold R. Harris, was the first man to save his life by making an emergency free fall parachute jump from a disabled aircraft. After bailing out, Harris did have difficulty in finding his rip cord and fell 2000 feet before he finally opened the chute at about 500 feet above the ground. The value of the free fall parachute had now been proven. One month later the Caterpillar Club was founded.
1925 **America**	Army instructor Steven Budreau, in an attempt to prove that the perils of long delayed falls could be eliminated through a technique of stabilizing the body, leaped from 7000 feet over Selfridge Field and fell free for 3500 feet prior to opening his parachute.
1928 **America**	In October, General Billy Mitchell arranged for six American military men to jump from a Martin bomber at Kelly Field, Texas, land, and set up a machine gun. Thus, the first paratroopers were born.
1930 **Russia**	The first sport parachute jumping was conducted at the Sports Festival in July of 1930. Contests were held by amateur jumpers — factory workers — to see who could land nearest to a selected target.
1932 **America**	As a result of Mr. Joe Crane's efficient organization and control of over 40 parachute contestants at the National Air Races, Roosevelt Field, N.Y., the National Aeronautic Association (NAA) agreed to sanction all formal sport parachuting competitions in the USA and appointed Mr. Crane to the NAA Board of Directors as its first parachuting representative, a position which he still holds. Also at this time Mr. Crane led a movement to obtain better conditions and contracts for professional parachutists which terminated in the formation of the National Parachute Jumpers Association (NPJR) the initial forerunner of the present Parachute Club of America.

1933 **Russia**	Osoaviakhim (The Society for the Promotion of Aviation and Chemical Defense) took over all sport parachute clubs and unified them into a national sport parachuting organization.
1933 **Russia**	Sixty-two parachutists jumped from three bombers in the first mass jump of parachutists.
1934 **America**	Experiments were initiated by the U.S. Forestry Service to drop men and supplies by parachute to fight forest fires. These men were later nicknamed "smoke jumpers," a name which stands today.
1934 **America**	Mr. Floyd Smith published an article in a commercial magazine which outlined techniques developed to control the body during delayed free falls. This technique was basically the same as those being used in sky diving today.
1936 **Russia**	By this date there were 559 parachute training towers in Russia and 115 parachute training stations.
1941 **America**	Arthur H. Starnes, a stunt-jumper, made a successful scientific and record breaking free fall from 30,800 feet to 1500 feet. Working with physiologists and doctors the jump was made to prove that properly equipped aviators could survive long delays from high altitudes without suffering any ill effects.
1948 **France**	The National Aeronautic Association, prompted by its parachuting delegate, Mr. Joe Crane, proposed that the Federation Aeronautique Internationale (FAI) recognize parachuting and establish parachute records commensurate with other aviation sports. As a result, the FAI created an International Parachuting Commission and Mr. Crane became the USA's first delegate.
1949 **France**	France earnestly took up parachuting as a sport (subsidized by the government as in the Soviet Union) and formed ten public sport parachuting centers throughout the country. In 1950 these same Frenchmen refined the true secret of today's free and delayed fall techniques and perfected the stabilized falling position.
1951 **Yugo-** **slavia**	The first international parachuting contest was held and won by France.
1955 **America**	Mr. Jacques A. Istel, after visiting France and watching the excellent parachuting being done by the Frenchmen, brought their sky diving techniques home to the U.S. and organized and trained the first U.S. sport parachuting team to compete in international competition.
1956 **Russia**	The first international U.S. sport parachute team competed at Tushino Airport, Moscow, using borrowed equipment and methods borrowed from France. The team scored sixth of ten nations competing.
1957 **America**	Under the leadership of Mr. Istel, the National Parachute Jumpers and Riggers Association was converted to the Parachute Club of America for the control and advancement of sport parachuting in the U.S.

SPORT PARACHUTING HAD ARRIVED IN AMERICA

1958 The U.S. Army completely reversed their anti-sport parachuting attitude and published regulations which not only permitted Army personnel to make sport parachute jumps but also called on commanders to foster and encourage the activity at all levels. Almost overnight, military clubs blossomed out at Army installations all over the country.

1958 The first U.S. eliminations to select a U.S. Parachute Team were held at Abbotsford, Canada. This team competed at Bratislava, Czechoslovakia, in the fourth world championships and placed sixth among 14 countries, beating out France, the early teachers of Americans.

1959 Mr. Dave Burt, ex-paratrooper, smoke jumper, and professional parachutist, combined parachuting and scuba diving into a new concept called "parascuba."
America's first commercial sport parachuting center, similar to a ski center, was opened by Jacques A. Istel at Orange, Mass. The center included complete parachuting facilities for student and experienced jumpers.

1959 The U.S. Parachute Team placed second in the Adriatic Cup Meet held in Tivat, Yugoslavia. Fourteen nations competed and the Army's Loy Brydon placed second overall, the highest placement thus far for the U.S. in international competition.

1960 Capt. Joseph W. Kittinger, Jr., USAF, stepped from the gondola of a balloon at 102,800 feet over New Mexico with only a six-foot stabilization chute and fell to 18,000 feet before the main parachute opened automatically, thereby establishing the world record for the longest delayed fall with stabilization device in history.

1960 All positions on America's 1960 Parachute Team were won by Army parachutists who competed at Sofiya, Bulgaria. The team finished fourth but Henry (Jim) Arender won America's first parachuting gold medal by placing first in the highly competitive style event. America also entered its first women into international competition in the persons of Barbara Gray of North Carolina and Sherrie Buck of California.

1961 A contingent of instructors from Parachutes, Inc., Orange, Mass., established the first U.S. international parachuting record. Jacques A. Istel, Nathan Pond, Lewis Sanborn, and William Jolly established a four-man group record for both a new day and night record from 1500 meters with delay. On the day record they averaged 13 feet, 7 inches from target center and the night record 14 feet, 1 inch. Both of these records were formerly held by the Soviet Union. The Army Parachute Team quickly followed the lead and several months later established nineteen new world records.

1961	Four Army men, Jim Pearson, Danny Byard, Loy Brydon, Dick Fortenberry and Jim Arender, a civilian, represented the USA in an international meet between France, the USA, the Soviet Union, and Bulgaria at La Ferte-Gaucher, France. For the first time in U. S. history the USA won all five first place trophies in an international competition.
1962	PCA organized and conducted the first parachute instructor-examiner school in order to implement its new national parachute instructor program. Nineteen candidates from various parts of the country participated in both classroom work and jumping sessions in Arizona to receive the first group of parachute instructor licenses issued in this country.
1962	PCA membership hit a new high of over six thousand members and there was an estimated 15,000 sport parachutists now in the United States.
1962	The USA hosted its first world parachuting competition at Orange, Mass. This was the 6th World Sport Parachuting Championships which involved 24 foreign countries. Two Americans swept individual honors when Henry (Jim) Arender won the gold medal for first place overall and Muriel Simbro won first place overall for women. Also, the U.S. Women's Team, consisting of Muriel Simbro, Carlyn Olson, and Nona Pond, took first place for overall team — and this was the first time that the USA had entered a full womens team!
1963 Russia	Two men attempted two new world parachute altitude records. Major Yevgeny N. Andreyev of the Soviet Union leaped from the gondola of a balloon at 80,000 feet and fell free to 2600 feet to establish a new world delayed free fall parachute record. His companion, Colonel Pyotr I. Dolgov was to open his parachute immediately after leaving the gondola and establish a record for a jump without delay; however, his suit equipment malfunctioned and he froze to death in the high atmosphere.
1963 France	Mr. Jacques A. Istel of the USA was elected President of the Parachuting Committee of the Federation Aeronautique Internationale, a position formerly held by the delegate from Czechoslovakia.
1963 USA	The Federal Aviation Agency published the first formal rules governing sport parachuting thereby recognizing that sport parachuting was firmly established in U.S. aviation.

THE LANGUAGE OF PARACHUTING

Like all other groups of specialists, parachutists have many strange sounding words in their vocabularies. It is most necessary that the novice become familiar with these terms in order to understand the workings of the parachute, to intelligently communicate with other jumpers, riggers, and pilots, and particularly, to describe the actions of both himself and his parachute.

A description of a jump could sound like this: "During relative work today, Jim made a poised exit while I made a door exit and we both stabled in about four seconds. I tried to catch him with a medium delta and when that didn't work, I tried a full delta and caught him. He was using a frog, but as I approached he went into a high spread, buffetted, and lost control, so I did a 180 and a delta. We were at twenty seconds and terminal so I pulled and blew three panels. At 1500 I cross-risered a bad oscillation and turned the gore into the wind and prepared to slip to the cross using everything the T-slot could give me."

Confusing? Not so once you get into the list shown below. These terms are listed in the general order of occurence during a jump.

Student Parachutist: Person with less than 25 free and delayed falls.
    falls.

Parachutist: Person with 25 or more free and delayed falls, including:
    15 stable delayed falls of at least 10 seconds

5 stable delays, at least 20 seconds
3 stable delays, at least 30 seconds, and landed within 50 yds. of target center on 5 jumps with delays of 20 or more seconds, and demonstrated ability to hold a given heading.

Jumpmaster: Normally the senior jumper in the aircraft, or the instructor in charge in the aircraft when jumping students.

Wind Streamer: A narrow length of weighted paper or cloth dropped prior to the jump to measure wind drift and to assist in selecting the proper exit point.

Spotting: Selecting the course to fly, directing the pilot, and selecting the correct ground reference point over which to exit from the aircraft.

Sky Diving: The art of exiting from an aircraft at a high altitude, stabilizing the body during a free or delayed fall, executing various timed turns, rolls, maneuvers, and loops, safely opening the parachute at a given time over a given ground point, and then manipulating the parachute so as to safely land on a specific ground target.

Sport Parachuting: The same as Sky Diving.

Military Parachuting: Low altitude, static line, mass, formation parachute jumping for specific tactical purposes.

Poised Exit: A departure from the aircraft wherein the jumper uses the steps, wheels, and wing struts to brace on to assist in gaining a stable position immediately as he leaves the aircraft.

Door Exit: A dive out of the aircraft without using any braces, steps, wheels, or struts, to assist in gaining a stable fall position on exit. Generally executed from larger and higher speed aircraft.

Static Line: The cord or webbing attached to a parachute which is hooked to the aircraft and automatically pulls open the parachute when the jumper leaves the aircraft.

Dummy Rip Cord Pulls: A static line training jump wherein the student simulates the pull of a rip cord by actually pulling a dummy rip cord handle attached to the harness for this purpose.

Free Fall: Jumping from an aircraft without any attachment between your parachute and the aircraft and delaying the opening. The parachute deploys only when the jumper pulls the release or rip cord.

Delayed Fall: Same as Free Fall.

Stable Fall Position: A face-to-earth, spread-eagled, arched, arms and feet spread body position which keeps a jumper from turning, spinning, or tumbling in the air.

Frog Position: A modified stable fall position with less arch and with the arms and hands forming a "U" or "W", as opposed to being wide spread, and the legs bent at the knees.

Delta Position: A modified stable fall position with the arms drawn back, similar to a delta winged aircraft.

Pointing: Maneuvering the body during a delayed fall from the point of aircraft exit to the correct point over which to open the parachute.

Turns: Moving the arms, legs, and body during delayed falls so as to turn in the desired direction. Turns are figured and discussed on the degrees of a complete circle. A half turn is a one-eighty, the full turn is a three-sixty. Two complete turns, one in each direction, is called a figure eight.

Terminal Velocity: The greatest speed at which a body falls through the atmosphere (14.7 psi). Resistance of the air overcoming the pull of gravity establishes the approximate figure of 176 feet per second or 120 mph which is reached after 12 seconds of delayed fall.

Tracking: Varying the body position into an inverted arch which offers maximum horizontal movement during the free fall while also increasing the rate of descent.

Relative Work: Two or more jumpers working together, during the delay period of a delayed fall, to execute coordinated body maneuvers, pass a baton, etc.

Opening Point: The ground point of reference over which the jumper opens his parachute to enable him to drift onto the center of the ground target.

Rip Cord: The handle and cord which holds the parachute closed until the jumper pulls it loose, thereby unlocking the back pack and permitting the parachute to deploy.

Sleeve: (also Deployment Bag) The device used to encase the parachute canopy which prevents the jumper from wrapping in the deploying canopy, creates drag thereby decreasing opening shock, and permits the orderly deployment of both suspension lines and canopy.

Parachute: (French word: para-meaning to guard against, chute-meaning a fall.) An apparatus used in descending safely through the air from a great height, particularly an aircraft. Umbrella like in form and rendered effective by the resistance of the air which expands it during the descent and then reduces the velocity of its motion.

Parachute Assemblies: See Section IV.

Opening Shock: The tug felt by the jumper as the canopy initially inflates.

Oscillation: A pendulum-like, tilting action of an inflated canopy during descent.

Drift: The movement of the parachute and jumper caused by external wind or internal escaping of air through blank, or open, gores or slots in the canopy.

Slipping: Maneuvering the parachute by pulling on certain control lines (risers) and slipping air out from underneath the hem or skirt of the canopy to guide its direction.

Malfunction: Any improper functioning of the parachute.

Parachute Landing Fall (PLF): The method of falling down on landing by which a jumper absorbs and spreads the landing shock on various parts of the body, thereby preventing injury.

Carlessness: An act forbidden to parachutists!

SECTION III

YOUR FIRST JUMPING ADVENTURE

Once you have decided to become a parachutist, the hardest job that you will have is to answer your friends question, "Why?". There are as many answers to this question as there are parachutists and more are anticipated as sport parachuting becomes more and more popular throughout the United States.

Why da Vinci designed his parachute, or Veranzio jumped from a Venician tower, or the Montgolfier Brothers went up in balloons with homemade parachutes, or Perry and Morten jumped from the first airplanes is an intangible that probably will remain undefined. Many psychologists will explain these deeds by the fact that men have needs and compulsions and that in doing certain things these needs are satisfied. However, what **were** the needs of these men? Certainly, in addition to their needs and compulsions, there was an undying spirit of adventure . . . a something that challenged them! And when one becomes acquainted with any group of parachutists today, a spirit of adventure and challenge, not unlike those adventurers of yesteryear, is a strikingly predominate characteristic.

So let it suffice to say that parachuting is an adventure . . . a thrilling adventure which is as stimulating and challenging and rewarding as any yet devised in our modern age.

Awakening on the morning of your first jump, there is a sharp awareness within you that today is different. At once you are excited, eager, tense and alert, but outwardly calm and, perhaps, a little too casual. The coffee tastes extra good while the usual eggs and bacon seem too much to eat, even though you are hungry.

On the way to the airport you notice things like the little flags in the filling stations fluttering in the wind (and you subconsiously compute the wind speed at three to five miles per hour!), that the tops of the trees are not moving very much (this is good!), that the slight morning mist has already burnt off but there is still a good deal of humidity in the air (the better to ease you down with . . .), and that it's a beautiful day and a beautiful day for jumping!

At the airfield you wheel into the parking slot, turn off the ignition, pause slightly thinking, momentarily, that maybe you'd better train just a little more????? Nope! Dismount from the car, slam the door, and turn to face the silvery line of aircraft parked on the hardstand. As you approach the airstrip the jump aircraft is warming up and you can see the neat row of parachutes laid out beside it. Your confidence rises as the jumpmaster greets you, and other students, busy with their jump equipment, welcome you to their group.

To take the edge off everyone the instructor runs the group through a few side straddle hops and arch exercises and then calls off the flight order of jumping. You are number one on the first flight . . . a position earned by being a fast learner and working hard through the ground training.

And this ground training now pays off as you almost automatically go about checking the equipment. First the back pack, then harness, links, fasteners, static line, pins, reserve chute, helmet, straps, goggles, boots tightly laced . . . everything's OK.

The order to don equipment comes and automatically you fling the vest-like pack over your shoulders and slide into the harness, quickly connecting the fasteners. The jumpmaster then checks you out from head to toes, front and back, and taps your helmet signifying that the equipment is correct.

As you move toward the plane butterflies develop in your stomach and your legs seem to need a little more guidance than normal. Climbing into the plane and settling into your seat, the dry fear and doubt lessens and you become aware of every movement, each jumper's comments, and the details that the jumpmaster is telling you . . . "remember, head back and arch, spread yourself wide, count slowly . . . don't rush . . ."

Inside the plane the crowding by other jumpers makes everything seem more friendly and familiar and the number two jumper starts a nervous banter which goes back and forth as you taxi to the take-off position. Seat belts fastened, the plane lunges down the runway and almost immediately you're airborne at last.

As altitude is gained the early morning city below you becomes radiant and clean, greens and browns blending together and the streets and houses have a scrubbed, neat look. Here and there kids look up and wave and the jumpmaster in the open door waves back.

Coming now over the target at twenty-two hundred feet you watch the instructor lean out and correct the pilot's approach heading, fling his wind streamer out into the blast, and then silently watch it until it has landed. He then selects the exact point over

16

which he will tell you to jump from the aircraft, directs the pilot, and then beckons you to sit in the open doorway!

Suddenly you realize that the next action will be YOU, jumping from this aircraft . . . 2500 feet above the ground! Your heart chugs into a little faster beat and your palms become slick against the cool metal as you look down on the mottled earth below. The plane levels off in a final target approach path, the jumpmaster makes a last check of the static line, moves you out onto the aircraft wheel, crouching, hands grasping the wing strut, and calls for the engine to be slowed. Braced under the wing of the plane, head forward into the cool prop wash you pause, face wrinkling from the wind force and blurring the groud detail below, coveralls being plucked at from a thousand places, and notice the target below. Out here the decision has been made . . . never to return to this aircraft again. Tense, every nerve tingling ⸱⸱ awaited signal to jump seems like it will never come when, suddenly, you feel a sting on your leg and a voice from far off shouts "Go!" Now! A slight hesitation . . . wondering . . . "Did he tap me?" Can I actually DO it!

Dazedly you feel the muscles of your forearms tighten over the strut, feet and legs suddenly throw themselves out behind you, your body arches stiffly into the wind, hands push away from the strut, and you're away . . . falling, down, wind rushing, faster, falling, down, the earth moving below you, dropping . . . flat to the ground . . . watching it in the distance, knowing that you're falling but feeling suspended, spread-eagled, high in the sky. The aircraft now fading slowly, wind rushing past your helmet, falling . . . free, FREE . . . for the first time in your life! Free, from the earth or the machines above it . . . free to just lie there, face down, and watch the world go by! Counting! ("don't forget to count . . . Slowly!") Falling, you dimly hear your voice . . . ". . . one thousand, two thousand, three thousand, four thousand . . . Fi . . ." And as the voice passes four thousand a swishing sound comes from the parachute stringing out from behind and, almsot simultaneously, a sharp tug, a blur, a patch of color, the sound of a sheet being flipped tells you that you no longer fall free, that you are swinging under and open chute . . . you are afloat!

In a wave of triumphal emotion and relief you look up to discover the most wonderful piece of colored nylon cloth ever beheld . . . a real guardian angel!

As the swish of the opening parachute dies away a peculiar silence settles around you . . . a total, strange silence broken only by the air whispering out of the canopy vents. Now suspended from your two thousand foot perch, feet hanging limp into the greens below, the earth appears even more beautiful than from the plane. After looking over the scenery for awhile you remember that a landing will be next and you hurriedly search for the target, check the drift, and maneuver the parachute so as to get as close to the center as possible.

As the ground slowly rises the jumpmaster's instructions flash through your mind . . . "head up, feet together, relax!." Relax? Now you notice that the ground is not only coming up but it is also moving and you turn the parachute in order to ease the landing shock by facing into the wind. A voice drifts from below . . . ". . . prepare to land." Here it comes! The greens and browns now blurring and blending under and toward you . . . prepare . . . you tense, relax, tense again, relax again . . . where in hell is it! The horizon blurs . . . the earth lunges . . . Wham . . . you hit, jar, fall, roll, tumble, jump up, run around the canopy, pull suspension lines and risers, collapse it, then stand and look at the nylon now laying limp at your feet. Suddenly you realize that you are on the ground again, safe, nothing hurts, you're breathing hard but you don't know why . . . and YOU jumped! You did it!

Other jumpers run over to congratulate you and welcome you to their ranks, pound your back, and help roll up the nylon that served you so well. And you find yourself asking if you can go again today for another jump . . .

When the jumpmaster lands he signals you the sought after thumbsup sign indicating that you did everything perfectly and that you're cleared for the second jump. Immediately you start planning . . . a few more, then free falls! Lets GO!

SECTION IV

PARACHUTES

1. GENERAL TERMS AND FUNCTIONING

All sport parachutes generally consist of six major parts: the pilot chute, sleeve, the canopy, the suspension lines, the pack and the harness, as shown in Figure 5.

The pilot chute is a small parachute attached to the top of the sleeve and is used to pull the sleeve and main canopy from the pack quickly. The canopy is the large inverted cup-shaped piece of silk or nylon cloth which slows and supports the descent of the parachutist. Suspension lines connect the canopy to the harness. The pack encloses the pilot chute, sleeve, canopy, and suspension lines for easy wearing, protection, and handling. There are many types of harnesses but all are an arrangement of nylon or cotton straps and metal fittings designed to hold the parachute to the jumpers body and provide him with a seat or sling during the descent.

Two devices are generally used to open the parachute: the rip-cord and the static line. The rip cord is used when the jumper wishes to open the parachute himself. The static line is a length of webbing which is hooked to the inside of the plane and automatically opens the parachute as the jumper falls away from the aircraft.

The illustrations shown in Figure 6 depict the general order of functioning of the back pack type parachute with safety sleeve.

All sport parachutists are required to wear two parachutes: a main back-pack and a reserve parachute. In case there is a malfunction of the main parachute, then the reserve is used. The reserve is worn on the chest and fastened to rings or snaps on the front of the main harness webbing. As with back-packs there are many varieties of reserve parachutes, but in general, all reserves

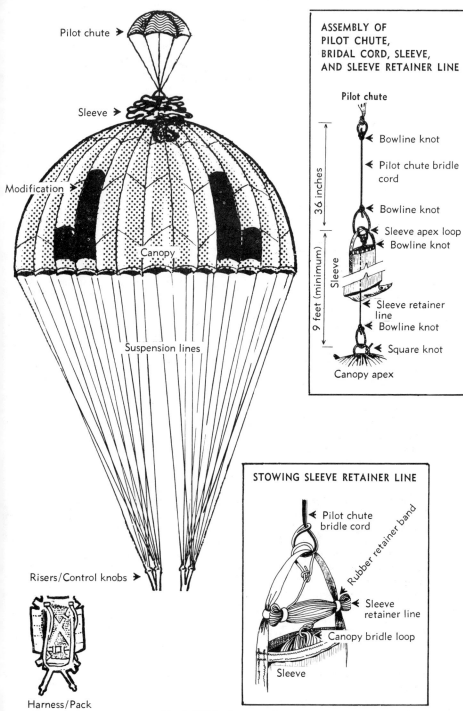

Pilot chute

Sleeve

Modification

Canopy

Suspension lines

Risers/Control knobs

Harness/Pack

ASSEMBLY OF PILOT CHUTE, BRIDAL CORD, SLEEVE, AND SLEEVE RETAINER LINE

Pilot chute

Bowline knot

Pilot chute bridle cord

36 inches

Bowline knot

Sleeve apex loop
Bowline knot

Sleeve

9 feet (minimum)

Sleeve retainer line
Bowline knot

Square knot

Canopy apex

STOWING SLEEVE RETAINER LINE

Pilot chute bridle cord

Rubber retainer band

Sleeve retainer line

Canopy bridle loop

Sleeve

Fig. 5, 6 Major Parachute Parts

20

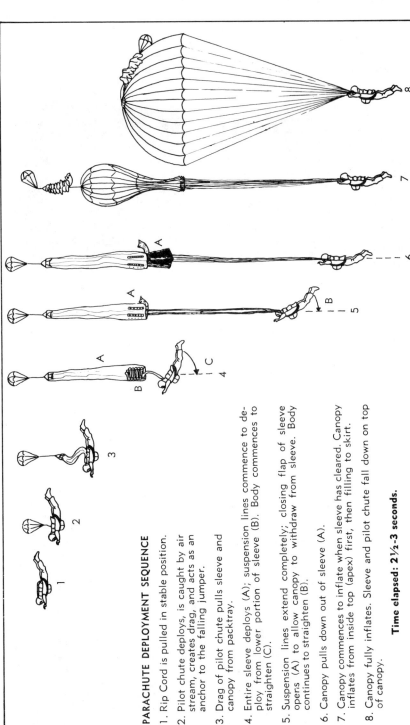

PARACHUTE DEPLOYMENT SEQUENCE

1. Rip Cord is pulled in stable position.

2. Pilot chute deploys, is caught by air stream, creates drag, and acts as an anchor to the falling jumper.

3. Drag of pilot chute pulls sleeve and canopy from packtray.

4. Entire sleeve deploys (A); suspension lines commence to deploy from lower portion of sleeve (B). Body commences to straighten (C).

5. Suspension lines extend completely; closing flap of sleeve opens (A) to allow canopy to withdraw from sleeve. Body continues to straighten (B).

6. Canopy pulls down out of sleeve (A).

7. Canopy commences to inflate when sleeve has cleared. Canopy inflates from inside top (apex) first, then filling to skirt.

8. Canopy fully inflates. Sleeve and pilot chute fall down on top of canopy.

Time elapsed: 2½-3 seconds.

Fig. 6, Canopy Deployment Sequence

are packed in small packs, have short rip cords, and function in the same manner as the main parachute. The two most popular types presently in use are as shown in Fig. 7.

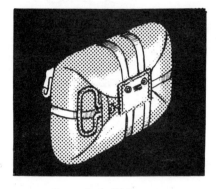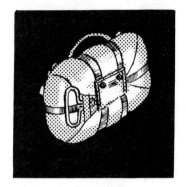

Square Pack, 28' Canopy   Barrel-Type Pack, 24' Canopy
Fig. 7, Reserve Parachutes

Another type of parachute is the seat-type; however, since this type is rarely used in sport parachuting, it has been omitted from this handbook.

Parachutes are designed and constructed with the old idea that a chain is only as strong as its weakest link. Each of the five major parts, from the lowest leg strap fastener to the top of the pilot chute, must be capable of carrying its share of the peak load which occurs during the initial opening shock.

Let's see how these sub-assemblies are made up.

2. PILOT CHUTES AND CANOPIES

The vane-type, coiled spring pilot chute is the favorite of sport parachutists due to the safety features therein. It is almost impossible to tangle or snag it since all suspension lines are enclosed within vanes and the coil spring itself sewn within the center core of the assembly. The pilot chute is made of the same nylon material as the main canopy. Figure 8 indicates the names of parts and shows the pilot chute construction.

Since Leonardo da Vinci the size, shape, construction, and design of parachute canopies has been a controversial subject—and even today men are still coming up with new ideas and modifications.

Three styles of canopies are in major use in the US today: the flat-circular type, the parabolic type, and the conical type canopy. Of these three, the flat-circular type is the most popular in sport parachuting. Major use of the parabolic chute is currently confined to Army parachute troops while the conical type is being employed in both Navy and Air Force high speed aircraft. Most of the discussions herein, except where otherwise noted, will pertain to the 28 foot circular type canopy.

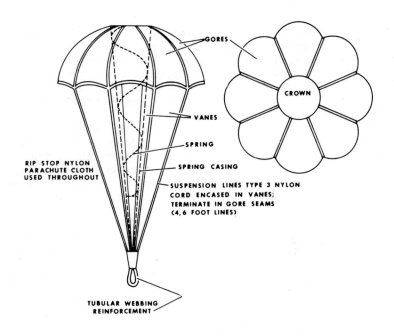

Fig. 8, Pilot Chute

This canopy is best described as a nylon polygon of 28 sides with a diameter of 28 feet—plus or minus 1 inch—constructed from 28 gores (like a pie sliced into 28 pieces) with each gore having four panels. This canopy requires approximately 796 square feet of nylon cloth connected by about 2400 yards of nylon thread in about half a million stitches. Construction of the canopy is as shown in Fig. 9.

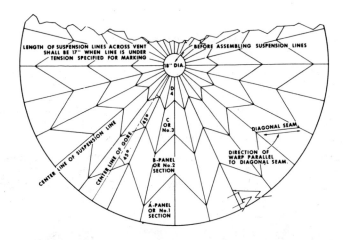

Fig. 9, Canopy Construction

Each gore is made up of four panels which are identified by the letters A, B, C, and D, starting at the skirt or bottom of the canopy. Diagonal seams are cut and sewn at a 45 degree angle to the centerline of the gore—known as bias construction—which provides maximum strength and elasticity. The skirt and vent hems are reinforced with 1 inch nylon webbing to insure that a tear does not completely separarte the canopy.

Suspension lines run continously from the lower connector link up through the canopy to the apex, then down to another lower connector link. In other words, there are 28 gores and 14 doubled over suspension lines which produce a count of 28 lines at the connector links. The canopy radial (or main) seams enclose the suspension lines in the channels produced by the stitching but are generally sewn to the canopy only at the skirt and vent seams. It takes about 75 feet of line to make the connection from link to link. The line itself is made up of a core of several nylon cords covered by a loosely woven nylon sleeve and the greatest strength comes from the inner cords. Figure 10 shows how the suspension lines are connected to the connector links and risers of the parachute assembly.

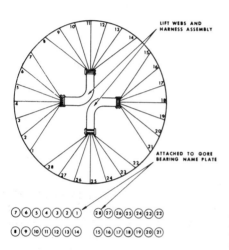

LIFT WEBS AND HARNESS ASSEMBLY

ATTACHED TO GORE BEARING NAME PLATE

Fig. 10, Connection of Suspension Lines

CANOPY MODIFICATIONS

In order to obtain maximum performance from canopies, in relation to better control in steering, many modifications have been made to the standard flat-circular canopy. The most popular of these modifications are shown in Figure 11 and all of these canopies have the characteristics of fast turns, a forward speed, and, when faced **into** the wind, reduced landing speed.

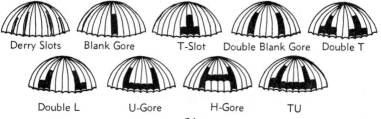

Derry Slots   Blank Gore   T-Slot   Double Blank Gore   Double T

Double L   U-Gore   H-Gore   TU

24

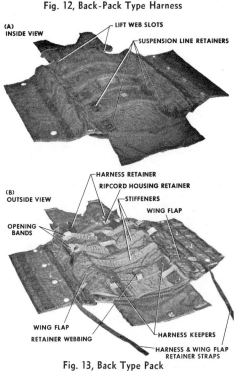

LIFT WEBS

CHEST STRAPS

CROSS SHOULDER STRAPS

BACK STRAP (date of m'f'g.)

MAIN SLING

LEG STRAPS

Fig. 12, Back-Pack Type Harness

3. HARNESSES

The main purpose of the harness is to form a sling in which the parachutist may sit or swing without any danger of separation from his parachute. The most popular back-pack harness today is one which is comfortable and can be quickly fitted to the individual wearer by easy adjustments. In the past fifteen years the harness has passed from a woven cotton webbing to a hard, tight weave nylon harness to today's model of a lightweight, soft weave nylon webbing which has a tensile strength of 1500 pounds in a strip 1½ inches wide. The major components of a back-pack type harness are as shown in Figure 12.

(A) INSIDE VIEW

LIFT WEB SLOTS

SUSPENSION LINE RETAINERS

(B) OUTSIDE VIEW

HARNESS RETAINER

RIPCORD HOUSING RETAINER

STIFFENERS

WING FLAP

OPENING BANDS

WING FLAP RETAINER WEBBING

HARNESS KEEPERS

HARNESS & WING FLAP RETAINER STRAPS

Fig. 13, Back Type Pack

Fig. 14, Locking Cones, Grommets, and Pins.

4. PACKS

The purpose of the pack is to house and protect the pilot chute, canopy, and suspension lines. To do this it must be rugged and durable. Today most packs are made of either canvas or nylon and machine stitched with nylon thread at 6 to 10 stitches per inch for strength. The general features found in most back packs are as shown in Figures 13 and 14.

5. RIP CORDS AND STATIC LINES

The rip cord is a manual releasing device containing pins which, when inserted into the pack locking cones, hold the pack closed. Normally it should take a pull of about 22 or more pounds to pull the pins out of the cones. The whole assembly is composed of a grip, a length of cable, and the necessary number of swaged pins. Most rip cord assemblies are proof-loaded to withstand a 300 pound pull. Some common rip cords are shown in Figure 15.

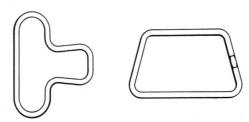

Used with:
Chest Type Parachute
Training Back Type Parachute
(Cloverleaf)

Used with:
Seat Type Parachute
Back-Type Parachute

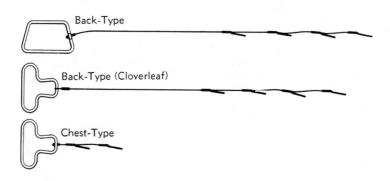

Back-Type

Back-Type (Cloverleaf)

Chest-Type

Fig. 15, Rip Cord Types

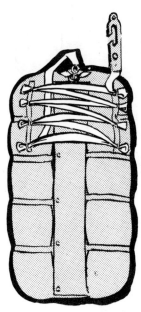

Fig. 16, Satic Line and Stow

In sport parachuting, static lines are used as a safety device to automatically open a parachute for beginning parachutists. Its components are a metal snap fastener which is hooked inside the aircraft, an eight foot length of nylon webbing, and a length of steel cable with swaged pins. The pins engage the pack locking cones as does the normal rip cord pins and the webbing is stowed across the back of the back pack. As the jumper leaves the aircraft, the webbing unfolds off the pack and then pulls the pins out of the locking cones, thus opening the pack and releasing the pilot chute. A static line and stow is as shown in Figure 16.

6. PARACHUTE INSPECTION, PACKING, AND CARE

The purpose of this portion on parachute packing and inspection is **not** to show a "do-it-yourself" method of packing parachutes since packing and rigging **must** be taught, in person, by a qualified instructor. It will, however, serve initially as a guide to familiarize you with packing procedures, particularly the sequence of packing, and later as a check list during actual packing.

The old safety slogan, "the life you save may be your own," could well sum up the story of a parachute packer! If there is one person that is hazardous to parachuting it's the happy-go-lucky, I-could-care-less parachute packer! Professional packers and riggers are required to be prepared to jump any parachute that they pack and sport parachutists could well adopt this rule. Another good rule to follow is, "if **you** are disatsified or unsure of **any part** of the packing job, repack it!"

There is quite a bit more to packing than just inserting a canopy into its pack. Actually, packing is a system, a combination of inspecting, rigging, and packing; and the perfect performance of a chute depends on the methods used in the system. All parachutes are packed essentially the same but will vary in the external rigging and internal placement.

In the beginning it will take quite long to properly pack a parachute; however, the time will shorten after a few weeks of practice. Remember, speed is secondary to accurary. A good packing method is to team up with a fellow jumper to work together in a two man packing team.

PACKING TOOLS

A good packer can assemble the common chutes without any tools; however, there are a few tools which do come in handy during the packing session. These tools can be made by you or purchased from most of the parachute manufacturing companies. A basic kit generally contains the items shown in Figure 17.

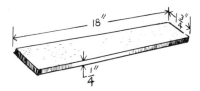

Packing Paddle (FID)

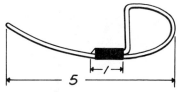

Temporary locking pin

Tension Board

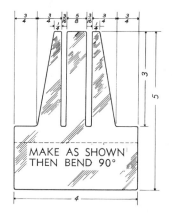

MAKE AS SHOWN
THEN BEND 90°

Fingers

Shot
Bags (3)

Fig. 17, Packing Tools

ENTANGLEMENTS

The first step in packing consists of removing any tangles in the suspension lines. These entanglements and twists are generally caused by the canopy or harness passing in between the suspension lines. The initial consideration in the methods employed to disentangle a fouled chute is to do it without damage to the suspension lines and canopy. On parachutes with canopy release devices, this is more easily done by removing the harness and pack.

Although many chutes may at times appear to be hopelessly tangled, your club instructor will quickly remove them using the following simple rules:

1. When the lines are knotted, remove the knots first.

2. Use the "rights and left" method, as shown by your instructor or rigger, to remove the simplest entanglements.

3. Work on only one group at a time, first a left, then a right. Start up from the pack, holding the fouled lines closest to the pack tray. Any number of suspension lines can be passed at the same time provided they are situated together.

4. Check all lines for clearance to the top gore of the canopy showing the nameplate. This nameplate must be readable on the outside of the gore, otherwise the canopy is inside out.

5. Once all lines are clear, check the proper rotation of the lines in relation to the canopy and connector links.

INSPECTION

After the entanglements have been removed, an inspection must be carefully conducted to insure air worthiness of the entire assembly. All of the various sub-assemblies must be inspected to insure that one part will not break or tear away from another and thus jeopardize the entire unit. When the ripcord is pulled the chute **must** function properly, quickly, and hold together during the opening shock. The time to inspect a parachute is **before** it is packed.

Unless you look specifically for imperfections, you may not find structural flaws and other details that cause malfunctions. When any flaws are found, no matter how minor, show them to your instructor or rigger before packing the chute. The major imperfections to look for are as follows:

WEAR: Look for chafing, tears, and bent or broken items. When these deficiencies are found it is important to consider **how** it occurred. Is it normal damage? If not, what happened, and why?

STAINS AND DETERIORATION: Foreign substances such as salt water, oil, grease, acids, and ammonia are harmful to parachutes and cause rapid deterioration. Stains caused by milder substances are a common indication of deterioration. **Any** stain can be a threat to safety and immediate steps must be taken by the rigger to detect, neutralize, and correct the trouble. All parts of the parachute must meet strength tests and once deterioration sets in a weaker performance must be expected.

SUSPENSION LINE CONTINUITY: Are all suspension lines in correct rotation both at the links and throughout the canopy?

INCOMPLETENESS: Is the entire assembly complete? Remember that any omission will affect the operation of the parachute and that an incomplete assembly could cause a complete malfunction.

MANUFACTURER'S ERRORS: If you purchase or use new equipment, have your instructor or rigger inspect it thoroughly before using. Newness does not insure perfection!

FLAWS: Nylon is a sturdy material and small flaws found in it may not affect its strength. However, whenever flaws are discovered, show them to the instructor or rigger for inspection and approval before packing.

Main parachutes must be repacked every 120 days. Reserve parachutes must be inspected and repacked at least every sixty days, even when they are not used. Remember, when in doubt, take the problem to an instructor or a rigger.

PACKING

Before proceeding further students are reminded that the packing of a backpack parachute for jumping should be done under the supervision of a qualified instructor or rigger and that the packing procedure shown below is merely a guide or checklist generally applicable to most parachutes. It is **not** complete in detailed procedure for any specific parachute.

Once the inspection has been completed, and the chute found to be free of defects, packing may commence.

To do this it is desirable to have a narrow, forty-foot, packing table; however, any large, smooth, clean surface, where tension can be applied to the parachute can be utilized. Contestants attending parachute meets have been known to pack their chutes in hotel hallways!

The parachute assembly should be under tension to be properly packed. This tension is applied by using a "spreader bar" to hold the connector links stationary at the harness end, a small hook looped through the apex at the peak end of the canopy, and then drawing the chute taut between the two.

After applying tension, a back-pack type parachute is then assembled in the following order of tasks:

1. Straighten the skirt hem by manipulating the suspension lines at the peak. Every effort should be made to straighten the skirt properly.

2. Whip and fold (sometimes called "flaking") the canopy to reduce the area of cloth to a series of neat, consecutive long folds.

3. Insert the suspension lines of each group into the respective slots of the suspension line holder and place a shot bag over the lines.

4. Straighten the bottom fold first and then all other folds.

5. Straighten each skirt hem and then align and count them to insure an equal number of folds on both sides.

6. Fold the canopy into thirds, longways, taking care not to disturb the skirt alignment and then place shotbags along the canopy to hold the folds.

7. Slide the sleeve over the canopy down to the canopy skirt, and straighten the sleeve closing flap.

8. Gently release the tension and unhook the connector links from the spreader bar.

9. The proper stowing of the suspension lines is the most difficult task in packing the parachute. The things to watch out for are twisted lines, dropped lines, uneven stowage, tearing the hesitator (retainer) loops and breaking rubber bands, and improper gauging of line length. Suspension lines are stowed on the lower portion of the sleeve and held in place by rubber retainer bands.

10. After the stows are complete the pack is then ready to receive the canopy. Place the canopy on the pack tray and accordion fold the canopy onto the container.

11. Position the pilot chute and prepare to close the pack.

12. While holding the pilot chute compressed and in place, bring up the side flaps and engage the flap grommets over the locking cones and insert two temporary locking pins into the two center locking cones.

13. Straighten the canopy, or sleeve fabric, and insert the locking cone on the top end flap through the corresponding pack grommet and insert the top rip cord pin.

14. Remove the temporary locking pins as the remaining rip cord pins are inserted into the locking cones.

15. Close the bottom flap and insert the last rip cord pin into the lower locking cone.

16. Insert the rip cord handle into the rip cord pocket. Straighten the endflaps using a packing paddle. Fasten the corner snaps, if applicable.

17. Hook up the elastic opening bands and fasten the rip cord protector flap.

18. Comply with your club instructions relative to signing packing records.

HANDLING — DO'S AND DON'TS

Do handle your parachute carefully and gently.

Do not pick it up by its risers or rip cord handle. Lifting or carrying a parachute by its rip cord handle will always result in a premature opening.

Don't place chutes near heat sources as heat causes nylon to become brittle.

Keep away from any dirt sources and grease and oils.

Dropping a parachute can bend or break the metal pieces and cause a complete malfunction.

Keep the parachute dry. Always keep it in a kit bag.

Don't place heavy objects on top of the parachute.

The best way to carry a parachute is to wear it without snapping the fasteners. Otherwise it should be carried in the kit bag or under the arm. Reserve or chest type parachutes should be carried by their carrying handles.

Take care of your parachute and your parachute will take care of you!

AIRCRAFT PROCEDURE, SPOTTING, AND EXITS

Almost any type of high wing aircraft can be safely used as a jump aircraft. Low wing aircraft can also be used by experienced parachutists; however, the exits are difficult and danger exists from a collision or entanglement with the tail sections of the aircraft. Low wing aircraft are definitely not recommended.

Characteristics of a good jump aircraft are as follows:

1. Capable of carrying a jumpmaster **and** one or more parachutists or students. (The more parachutists a plane can carry, the more jumps can be made and, generally, the cheaper the aircraft rental or operation fees.)

2. Have exterior steps and struts to assist the jumper in quickly obtaining a stable spread position upon leaving the aircraft.

3. Have a fast rate of climb to gain altitude in order to reduce the flying costs incident with high altitude jumps.

4. Have a secure fixture on which to fasten the static line snap fastener.

5. Have the capability to slow up to approximately 50-60 knots without deviating from course or quickly losing altitude.

Jumpmasters and instructors will thoroughly check the aircraft prior to jumps for any protruding hazards or unsafe conditions which would be unsafe for the jumpers. If a hazard cannot be removed, it is generally taped over to prevent snagging.

The aircraft is loaded in the reverse order of jumping.

Pilots are in full command of the aircraft at all times and the jumpmaster or instructor will work out emergency procedures and method of exiting jumpers with the pilot prior to taking off. Once the plane is underway, no movements are made within the aircraft unless so ordered by the pilot or jumpmaster. Seat belts are fastened prior to take off and smoking is not allowed on either take off or landing. Actually, it is a good procedure not to smoke at all on routine short jump flights due to the close conditions in the aircraft.

SPOTTING

Spotting is the correct selection of the exit point. At its best it is only an estimate and the jumper should be prepared to make changes in his course both during the delayed fall and after the parachute has opened.

The reason for spotting is to insure an exit from the aircraft over the best spot to take advantage of the wind currents in order that you may land on the center of the ground target.

For the purposes of this section, 2500 feet is used as the altitude where the jumper must open his parachute and then drift down onto the target. It is the open parachute drift that is the most important, although the drift encountered during the delayed fall does have an effect on spotting.

To measure the drift that will be encountered after opening the parachute, the plane, on its first pass, is flown into the wind directly over the center of the ground target at exactly 2500 feet actual altitude. As the plane centers on the target, the jumpmaster throws out a long narrow cloth or paper wind drift indicator, commonly called "the streamer," which will fall and drift at approximately the same rate as the parachutist. The jumpmaster watches the streamer until it lands and also times its descent to insure that it has fallen at the correct speed. Based on where the streamer lands, in relation to the target, the jumpmaster selects a point exactly the same distance opposite the target from where the streamer landed and in line with the target-streamer line. This point then is the exit point.

To insure that he has selected the correct ground reference exit point, the jumpmaster has the pilot bring the plane around and on a course over the streamer-target-exit point line as he climbs to the necessary altitude required for the first jumper. When the plane centers over the point where the streamer landed he starts his stopwatch and as he centers over the target he notes the time elapsed. The same amount of seconds opposite and in line with the streamer-target line should be the exit point and he rechecks and adjusts, if necessary, the ground reference exit point.

If the exit point is correct, the altitude correct, and the jumper ready, the first exit is then made. Figure 18 is a schematic diagram of how the wind indicator is used to select the exit point.

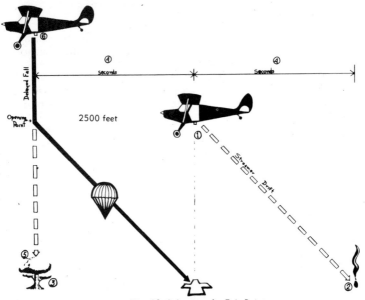

Fig. 18, Selecting the Exit Point

1st Pass: 1—Drop streamer over center of target, 2500'.
2—Observe and time where streamer lands downwind of target.
3—Select a ground reference exit point the same distance upwind and on the same line that the streamer landed downwind.
2d Pass: 4—Time distance from streamer to target and target to selected exit point.
5—Select exact ground reference point.
6—Exit parachutist over exit point.

CAUTIONS:

1. The wind indicator method is not an **exact** calculation.
2. Winds vary. The streamer may have drifted horizontally in this manner:

or vertically in this manner:

Fig. 20, Vertical Streamer Drift Example

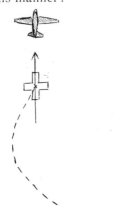

Fig. 19, Horizontal Streamer Drift Example

3. On aligning the aircraft, sight over the door edge but always keep head in same position when aligning and

34

sighting to avoid error. Check to insure that the plane is level, otherwise you will be off target as shown below:

Fig. 21, Insuring Level Aircraft

4. Remember, as you approach the target, that the pilot can no longer see the ground panels. Direct him by indicating right or left so many degrees. Work these signals out prior to leaving the ground.
5. Throw the streamer outward and downward to avoid hooking it on the aircraft tail sections.

The step-by-step sequence of

EXITS

Leaving the aircraft is generally done in one of two ways: a poised exit or a door exit.

In the poised exit the jumper sits in the open doorway, places his feet on a special step or the actual step and wheel, pulls himself out of the doorway and grasps the wing strut, then, bracing on the strut, thrusts his feet up and rearward until the legs and body are parallel with the aircraft, and finally, gently pushes backward from the strut into the spread-eagled, stable fall position. The poised exit should be the only exit method used in static line jumps.

In the door exit the jumper crouches in the doorway, swings himself out from the doorway toward the front of the aircraft, assumes the stable fall position face to earth, and aligns himself with the flight path of the aircraft. Another door exit is to dive toward the rear of the aircraft and immediately assume a delta spread position.

Needless to say, it is more difficult to quickly gain and maintain a stable fall position via the door exit than from the poised exit and students are cautioned to master the poised exit prior to attempting door exits.

a poised exit is as shown in Figure 22.

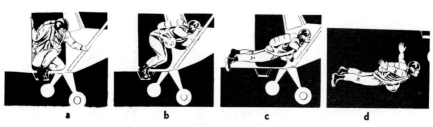

a   b   c   d

Fig. 22, Poised Door Exit

The Method of making a door exit is as shown in Figure 23.

Fig. 23, Door Exit

Remember, the main objective of all exits is to gain and maintain a stable fall position as quickly as possible. This will also permit immediate observation of the ground references and enable the parachute to deploy **above** the jumper without the possibility of interference from the body.

In competitive jumping, points are lost when the jumper fails to stabilize within a certain period of time after leaving the aircraft.

Lastly, the stabilized position permits the jumper to fall at a uniform rate of speed to conform with the predetermined calculations timed by his stopwatch.

SECTION VI

STABLE FALL POSITIONS
TURNS, RIP CORD PULLS, COUNTING and TIMING

Anyone can throw themselves out of an aircraft and fall, but not everyone can control themselves during this period of fall. To do this takes coordination, thinking, and determination. Man used to think that he would "black out" during a fall of any length. This thought has long since been pushed into the category of the old wives tale. Then for many years it was thought that when he did fall he would just twist, roll, tumble, and turn, powerless to control himself. This, too, has now been proven otherwise. Not only can he stablize and control his fall, he can maneuver himself through the air, control some of his falling speed, execute rolls and loops, and maneuver his body horizontally above the earth in any direction he wishes to go! And this he does by arm, leg, and body movements.

The first thing that a sky diver must learn is to stabilize his body throughout his falling period without losing control. This is done by assuming the basic stable spread position immediately upon exiting the aircraft as shown in Figure 24.

In the basic stable spread position the head is thrown back, eyes on the horizon. Holding the head back helps to arch the back. The chest is raised and arched as in the military position of attention.

The arms are spread wide and in line with the shoulders. Hands are relaxed, fingers spread wide. The back is arched as far as the confirmation of the body will allow-strain! Legs are comfortably spread, equally level, knees slightly bent. Feet are equally level.

Fig. 24

Fig. 25

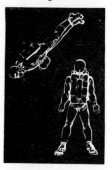

Fig. 26A

Fig. 26B

Another stable position is called the "French Frog" position and is shown in Figure 25.

The frog position is a flat position as compared with the basic stable arched position. Head is straight, eyes at a 45 degree angle from fall axis. Chest is raised and arched. Arms are bent with hands at shoulder level and in line with shoulders. Legs are spread and equally level. Knees slightly bent.

The Delta position is another stable position but one which gives the jumper a forward glide coupled with a slight dive. It is the same as the basic stable fall position with the exception of the arms which are drawn back in towards the sides at about a 45 degree angle, similar to the outer wing edges of a delta winged aircraft. With the arms at a 45 degree angle the position is known as a medium delta and at about 30 degrees, a full delta. The delta position is shown in Figure 26 A and B.

Once the basic stable fall positions have been perfected to where the jumper can gain and maintain his stability, preferably for delayed falls up to at least 15 seconds, he should then commence to learn the turns.

It is necessary to be able to turn in order to place yourself directly over the correct opening point. Spotting the exit point can not always be accomplished in the manner desired, thus, after a long delay when you find that you are off your opening point, you can turn and maneuver yourself to where you can correctly open the parachute.

Turns are most easily learned initially by looking in the direction that you wish to turn and then dropping or lowering that arm and shoulder. This will cause a slow turn in the direction of the arm dropped. Inclining the upper part of the body into the direction of turn will assist in turning and will add to the speed of the turn. After these slow turns have been mastered, the turning speed may be increased even further by increasing the dip of the shoulder (Fig. 27) (the one on the turning side), raising the opposite arm, and drawing up the leg on the same side of the body. (Fig. 28)

Turns are not immediate with body movement and the student should be prepared to hold the turn position until it takes effect. The same holds for stopping the turns, thus the jumper should stop the turn just **prior** to reaching the heading on which he wishes to remain.

A complete 360 degree turn to the right, followed by a complete 360 degree turn to the left, is called a "figure eight." This maneuver is generally required in most parachuting competitions.

Figure 28A depicts the position for back-to-earth stable position. The limbs must remain symmetrical spreadeagled as in the face-to-earth position, but in this case the body is bent at the waist rather than arched.

Figure 28B shows the Cannarozzo position. The head-down attitude requires a good deal of skill to remain stable in the position. Rate of descent (terminal velocity) also increases greatly.

Other maneuvers, such as front and back loops, barrell-rolls, etc., are within the capability of the parachutist; however, these should be learned directly from a qualified instructor.

It is strongly recommended that the arched basic stable fall position be learned first, followed by other positions. All positions have their place and merit and can be successfully used during any one jump, particularly when maneuvering with other parachutists in the air during relative work. The student should not proceed into turns or advance work until the ability to **consistently** stablize has been proven. To do so is hazardous!

RIP CORD PULLS

Along with perfecting the stable fall, it is necessary to become proficient at pulling the rip cord without losing control of the stabilized position. Naturally, this starts during the static line training by making dummy rip cord pulls.

Like all movements, the pull should be made quickly and smoothly. **Both** hands should be brought into the ripcord handle simultaneously, the handle grasped with the right hand and pulled, and both hands and arms returned to the outstretched position. Just as the jumper moves his hands in for the pull he should force his body into an extreme arch, force his head back and chin in, and lower his eyes to **look directly at the rip cord handle.** The head and trunk will generally lower somewhat during this movement but will level off as soon as the spread position is resumed.

Fig. 27

Fig. 28

Fig. 28A

Fig. 28B

39

Losing control on rip cord pulls causes parachute malfunctions, damage to the parachute, delayed openings, and injuries. Hunching the shoulders or a slow pull will cause the jumper to flip completely over during the pull period and perhaps cause the feet to become entangled in the suspension lines. After the main chute has opened, the rip cord (don't drop it—point of honor!) can be tucked under an opening band of the reserve parachute.

Caution: Sometimes when a perfect stable fall position is held throughout the pull, the pilot chute will not clear the negative pressure area which has built up over the jumpers back and will "flutter" or hesitate on top of the open pack tray. It is for this reason that a count is necessary after the rip cord has been pulled. When this occurs, merely dip either shoulder toward the ground which will break up the negative pressure area and allow the air stream to catch the pilot chute and deploy the canopy.

COUNTING AND TIMING

Pulling the rip cord brings up the questions of **when** to pull it and how you will know when this critical moment has arrived. Three systems are generally used to time or mark your delayed fall period: verbal counting, use of a stop watch, and use of an altimeter, or any combination of the three.

The verbal count is fairly accurate for persons who practice often while using a watch with a second hand to time themselves. The counting should be done aloud both in practice and actual use. There will be a tendency during the actual fall to speed up the count. The normal method used is to count by thousands, to say, "one-thou-sand, two-thou-sand, etc." at the normal speaking rate. Saying it in this manner takes one second for each one-thousand said.

When you make your first static line jumps, the verbal count should be used so that you can learn to count correctly and also save yourself the extra chore of watching instruments and allow you to concentrate more fully on the body position and arch. Also, the count is used to determine if the main chute has opened at the proper time. If it hasn't opened in the allotted time, emergency procedure should be initiated immediately to activate your reserve.

During delayed falls, the count is used both to time the delay period **and** time the opening after the rip cord pull. For example, if you are going to delay for five seconds and then pull the rip cord, you should count by thousands up to five-thousand, pull, and **continue** the count for the number of seconds that your instructor informs you it will take for the parachute to inflate.

It is recommended that the verbal count be replaced by a stop-watch or an altimeter, or both, for delays over eight seconds, since instruments are more accurate than the verbal count.

When the stop watch and/or altimeter is used, it is mounted on a bracket which fits onto the reserve parachute where it can be easily read during the fall. Many devices can be used to safely mount these instruments; however, they should be carefully checked prior to a jump to insure that they do not impede the deployment of the

Fig. 29, Example-Instrument Panel

reserve parachute should it be needed. Figure 29 shows a reserve with one type of altimeter - stop watch plate affixed thereto.

When the altimeter is used, great care should be taken to insure that it is correctly set prior to boarding the aircraft. Once aloft, it should again be checked against the aircraft altimeter to insure that it is functioning properly.

DISTANCE FALLEN IN FREE FALL STABLE SPREAD POSITION

This table is computed for Free Fall in the Stable Spread (Face to Earth) position for an opening altitude of 2500 feet above drop zone and for average summer temperatures and pressure conditions.

CAUTION: The rate of descent increases with (1) other body position, (2) higher temperatures, (3) lower pressure (e.g. higher field elevation). Use this table with extreme caution at field elevations over 1000 feet, especially during long delays. Always add 200 feet extra for each 1,000 of field elevation.

Distance Fallen Per Second up to Terminal Velocity		Distance Fallen in Free Fall Stable Spread Position Cumulative Distance in Feet									
Sec	Dist	Sec	Dist	Sec	Dist	Sec	Dist	Sec	Dist	Sec	Dist
1	16	1	16	13	1657	25	3745	37	5833	49	7921
2	46	2	62	14	1831	26	3919	38	6007	50	8095
3	76	3	138	15	2005	27	4093	39	6181	51	8269
4	104	4	242	16	2179	28	4267	40	6355	52	8443
5	124	5	366	17	2353	29	4441	41	6529	53	8617
6	138	6	504	18	2527	30	4615	42	6703	54	8791
7	148	7	652	19	2701	31	4789	43	6877	55	8965
8	156	8	808	20	2875	32	4963	44	7051	56	9139
9	163	9	971	21	3049	33	5137	45	7225	57	9313
10	167	10	1138	22	3223	34	5311	46	7399	58	9487
11	171	11	1309	23	3397	35	5485	47	7573	59	9661
12	174	12	1483	24	3571	36	5659	48	7747	60	9835

HOW TO CALCULATE JUMP ALTITUDE FOR DELAYED JUMPS

1. Select length of delay.
2. Find distance fallen in free fall in this time from table.
3. Add 2500 feet for opening altitude.
4. The total is your jump altitude above the ground where you set altimeter.
5. Remember to check that the aircraft altimeter is set for field elevation on takeoff.
   SUGGESTED SAFETY RULE: Add 200 feet to jump altitude for each 1000 feet of field elevation. Remember, your terminal velocity is greater at high altitudes.

EXAMPLE (1)	**EXAMPLE (2)**
Thirty second delay from field with elevation of 300 feet.	Twenty second delay from field with elevation of 3200 feet.
Distance fallen in 30 seconds 4615 ft	Distance fallen in 20 seconds 2875 ft
Add 2500 feet for opening altitude 2500 ft	Add 2500 feet for opening altitude 2500 ft
JUMP ALTITUDE 7115 ft	Safety margin—3x200 feet 600 ft
	JUMP ALTITUDE 5975 ft

Fig. 30, Delayed Fall Time Chart (Reproduced with permission of Parachutes, Inc.)

The favorite of sport parachutists today is to use both the stop-watch and altimeter mounted on a plate or board. Each can be used to check the other. Also, since the body falls faster or slower when out of control or unstable, the stopwatch would not then indicate the correct altitude as previously computed from the delayed fall time chart and the altimeter could be used to judge the opening altitude.

The delayed fall time chart shown in Figure 30 can be used to compute the exit altitude for the various desired delays.

In using the stop watch, the jumper waits until he is ready to exit the aircraft and, at the last moment, punches its activator and then departs. If the aircraft configuration requires a few seconds in which to climb onto the wing strut prior to exit, then this amount of time should be allowed for in the overall timing. It may also help the jumper to place a small piece of colored tape over the numbers on both the stopwatch and altimeter numbers on which he will make his rip cord pull.

AIR, GRAVITY, AND FRICTION

It is generally well known that the higher you go the less air there is. Stated in weight measurements this means that air pressure causes one cubic foot of air at sea level to weigh .08 of a pound and that the same cubic foot of air at higher levels would contain less air and thus weigh less.

If there were no air, all things would fall at the same rate of speed, pulled down by the gravitational pull of the earth. This gravitational speed is always 32 feet per second, per second which means that during the first second of fall an object would achieve a speed of 32 feet per second, 64fps during the second second, 96 feet per second at the end of the third second, and so on.

However, there is air and it must be remembered that for every motion there is a friction created. When an object falls from a height, gravity pull will cause it to fall faster each second and the faster it falls, the more friction it creates by moving through the air. (The higher the air, the greater the speed and the less the friction; the lower the air the greater the friction and the less the speed.) Friction increases with the square of the speed. The faster an object moves through the air the more friction it creates and the more it is slowed! Are you still there?!

Sooner or later the speed and friction will balance each other and when the balance of these two forces is reached, the falling object will then have reached a steady falling speed which is called terminal velocity. In atmosphere this takes about 12 seconds and is approximately 176 feet per second or 120 miles per hour. Once terminal velocity is reached, an object will not fall any faster. Terminal velocity is a higher rate of speed at 30,000 feet than it is at 2000 feet due to the lesser friction of air at the higher altitude. As a falling parachutist passes from the higher thin air into the lower dense air, his friction would increase and the terminal velocity slowed.

Body position in the air also effects speed. If a parachutists dives straight down at the earth, the position of his body would offer little resistance (approximately $1\frac{1}{2}$ square feet) to the air and would cause him to fall faster. Conversly, if he fell flat and spread his arms and legs, he would offer about ten square feet of body surface to resist the air and thus slow his fall.

Forward speed is another consideration in parachuting. When a jumper leaves an aircraft which is traveling at 100 miles per hour he also continues to move in the same path as the aircraft. If there were no air he would continue to move through the air at the same 100 miles per hour until he hit the ground. Again, however, there is air, and his forward path is slowed and, finally, stopped by friction.

In summary, a parachutist jumping from a moving aircraft will continue to move forward as he falls, will increase his falling speed until friction balances speed at terminal velocity, and terminal velocity will be greater in higher altitudes than in lower altitudes. Body position can speed up and slow down the falling speed.

As the falling parachutist pulls his rip cord and deploys the 28 foot, flat circular canopy, he increases his ten square feet of air resistance with approximately 796 square feet of nylon cloth. This upside down cup-shaped canopy offers maximum resistance as it moves downward through the air at approximately 16 feet per second. Both the forward and downward free fall motion are checked by the parachute opening.

Needless to say, the greatest strain on the parachute comes during the opening when the falling speed is sharply reduced. The major factors in determining the exact strain during the opening are the speed of the plane, the distance fallen, the altitude, the weight of the man, and the type of deployment aid, such as a safety sleeve or a deployment bag.

Since most parachutes are designed for stresses of approximately 8000 pounds, there is relatively little danger of the parachute being rendered useless by the opening shock.

As the parachute descends it grabs and compresses the air within the canopy and maintains air pressure against its inner surfaces. Some of this air escapes up through the apex vent hole and some through the cloth itself, while other air spills from under the skirt hem of the canopy. The air escaping upward through the vent hole reduces oscillation and holds the canopy steady.

Also effecting the canopy are horizontal winds which push the chute along (drift), vertical up-currents which cause the canopy to rise or slow the descent, and downdrafts which hasten the landing.

In summary, the parachute resists, drags, and compresses air while combining a balance of air density, weight, area, and cloth porosity to produce a safe descending speed for the parachute jumper.

SECTION VIII

PARACHUTE MANIPULATION

When you pull your rip cord, the opening of the main parachute will reduce your falling speed to 16 feet per second. And this will take from 1½ to 3 seconds, depending on the free falling speed attained prior to the pull.

Your first action after feeling the parachute open is to look up and **check your canopy** to insure that the canopy has inflated correctly and that there are no parachute malfunctions.

Your next actions, in order, should be to locate the target and then determine the direction and speed of your drift. Then, keeping the location of the target in mind, make corrections to counteract the changing winds and gusts which will probably effect your drift at different altitudes.

For those jumpers using a standard flat circular canopy, without any of the modifications shown in Section IV, movements are generally limited to the various slips. However, those with canopy modifications, can slip, turn the canopy, and maneuver both fast and far.

SLIPS

To slip a parachute means to pull down on certain risers and suspension lines which causes the air to spill out of the opposite side of the canopy. This action provides a slipping motion of the canopy through the air in the same direction as the group of lines pulled. In other words, pull down on the right side group and you will slip to the right, as shown in Figure 31. It must be remembered that slipping will increase your rate of descent and

45

should be avoided once you have prepared to land. Manipulation of the lines and releasing the slip too quickly often cause oscillations which can be dangerous when landing.

To execute a normal slip, reach up as high as possible on the two risers you desire to pull and then pull them down until your hands are centered on your chest. The further down you pull the suspension lines, the faster the rate of descent. Make a sharp initial pull to more effectively spill air from the canopy. During the slip, look in the direction the slip is being made. After completing the slip, let up the risers slowly to avoid oscillation.

TURNS

In addition to slipping, parachute canopies that have blank gores, etc., can be turned by using the turning devices generally located on the rear risers as shown in Figure 32.

Step 1   Step 2
Fig. 31, Right Slip

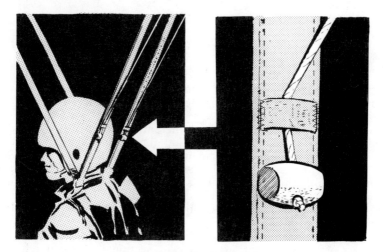

Fig. 32, Canopy Turning Devices

These canopies move through the air at approximately six to eight miles per hour—a horizontal speed caused by compressing air being forced out of the opening in the canopy which pushes the parachute in the opposite direction of the opening, similar to air released from a toy balloon.

By pulling down on the turning devices, which are connected to the suspension lines on either side of the canopy openings, the air flow from the slots is changed (turned) and forces the canopy to turn in the direction of the turning line pulled. In other words, to turn the canopy to the right, the right turning device is pulled

46

downward and held until the desired degree of turn is completed. Like a slip, these turning devices must also be let up slowly in order to avoid oscillation. A complete 360 degree turn can generally be completed in from 4 to 6 seconds, depending on the amount and placement of the canopy slots or blank gores.

MANEUVERING

The main reason for maneuvering the parachute in sport parachuting is to land on the center of the ground target. Since wind speed and direction cannot be accurately determined, and humidity varies with elevation, a jumper can rarely select an opening point from where he will not have to maneuver his parachute in order to land on the target. Wind gusts and changes in wind direction are the jumpers biggest headaches. These conditions can change themselves almost completely in a matter of minutes.

Once the jumper has checked his canopy, he determines his speed and direction of drift in relation to the target by observing which direction the earth is moving beneath his feet. For example, if the target is close under his immediate front and he is drifting fast toward the target, a turn of 180 degrees should be made to face the jumper away from the target. If he continues to drift toward the target, he should then slip to his front or away from the target.

All this time he should closely watch the target and check the drift by watching his feet in relation to the ground.

A good rule to follow is always try to stay upwind of a target. This will allow him to come in on the target at the last minute; however, if the wind dies, he will then land short of the goal. But, if the jumper once allows himself to be blown downwind, then he must work into the wind for the remainder of the descent and most of the time this is a losing battle.

Normally during descent, with the open gore canopy, the jumper should face into the wind. This will cut down his wind drift by about six miles per hour. Conversely, if the jumper faces with the wind, his speed will increase to wind speed plus six miles per hour!

Landing **with** the wind with an open gore parachute **increases** the landing speed while landing facing the wind will decrease landing speed. It would be well for you to memorize and **use** the following rule: Face into the wind on landing!

Using the diagrams in Figure 33, next page, think what your maneuvering actions would be in each case to place yourself onto the center of the target. Check your solutions with your instructor.

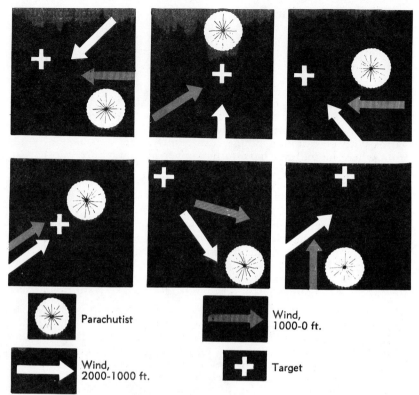

Fig. 33, Parachute Maneuvering Diagrams

SECTION IX

LANDINGS

"One thousand!" The length of time that it takes to say those words is the same length of time that you will have to start, make, and complete your landing by parachute. Not much time to think or make any changes in landing plans, is it!

What it boils down to then is that landings must be practiced over and over again and perfected **before** you make your first jump. The parachute landing fall (PLF) must practically become a habit and executed automatically on landing. A good landing is one that you walk away from! Most of the minor injuries in sport parachuting are caused during incorrect landings.

During WW II many different types of landing falls and tumbling were tried by the military forces in order to develop the safest method for parachutists to hit the ground. The landing falls shown and described herein are the ones which were finally adopted and have been proven during millions of parachute jumps. It is particularly important that student parachutists learn, use, and perfect this technique of landing to insure continuous jumping through the early training period.

PREPARATION TO LAND

By the time you have descended to treetop level or approximately fifty feet above the ground, you should have selected your landing spot and started preparations to land.

In preparing to land, first extend your hands straight up and grasp both **pair** of risers with each hand. Hold the head up with eyes fixed on the horizon. If you look at the ground there is a tendency to either lift the feet up or stiffen the legs on impact.

Hold the feet and knees together, knees slightly bent, and toes pointed slightly downward to insure that the balls of the feet strike the ground first.

Relax the body as much as possible while maintaining sufficient muscular tension in your legs to insure that your feet and knees remain together during the fall. This will prevent your legs from collapsing and allowing the buttocks to receive the major landing impact!

On contact, execute the landing fall, in the direction dictated by the position of the body with respect to the line of drift. Recover immediately and collapse the canopy.

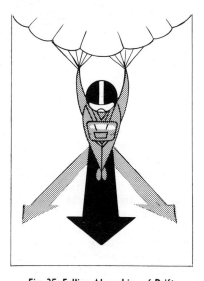

Fig. 35, Falling Along Line of Drift

Fig. 34, Prepare to Land Position

PARACHUTE LANDING FALLS (PLFs)

The parachute landing fall, Figure 36, is an exact method of landing which permits the parachutist to distribute the shock of landing throughout his entire body and thus reduce the chances of injury. When the body is moderately tensed, the muscular system is more capable of absorbing the landing shock than is the bone structure, much as a damp dishrag would be more capable than a dry stick. Bone joints must be unlocked by slightly bending the

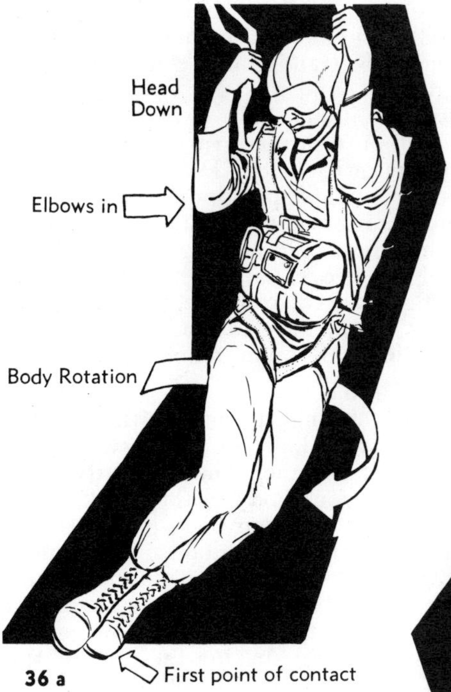

Head Down

Elbows in

Body Rotation

36 a   First point of contact

Continue Rotation

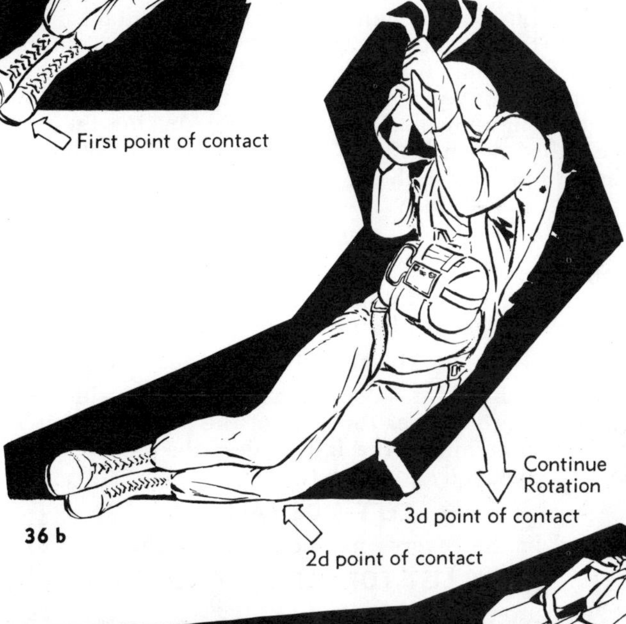

36 b

3d point of contact

2d point of contact

36 c

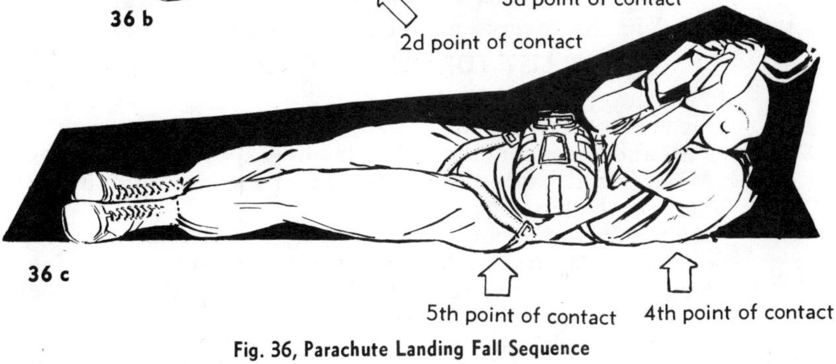

5th point of contact   4th point of contact

Fig. 36, Parachute Landing Fall Sequence

51

legs to prevent these joints from receiving a sharp jolt on landing. A fast recovery from the PLF should also be practiced so that the jumper will quickly regain his feet and collapse the parachute in order to avoid being dragged by wind gusts.

In learning PLFs the student jumps onto a mat or soft or grassy area from a two or three foot high platform. When the student is on the platform, the instructor calls READY, at which time the student assumes the prepare to land position by raising his arms overhead, closing his hands as if grasping the parachute risers, holding his knees together slightly bent, and holding his ankles and toes together, keeping his head erect, eyes on the horizon. At the command GO, he springs straight away from the platform onto the mat or landing area keeping the prepare to land position, and executes the predesignated landing fall upon touching the mat.

FRONT FALL

Assume the READY position, facing the mat with the toes extended over the edge of the platform. On GO, jump away from the platform, keeping knees and feet together, knees slightly bent. As the feet strike the ground, rotate your body to the right or left to avoid falling on the knees and to permit your body to absorb the landing shock on the following **five points of contact,** in sequence: the **feet, calf, thigh, buttock,** and **push-up muscle** (muscle behind your shoulder) as shown in Figure 36. The fall should be made in a fluid continuous motion with each point of contact following the other rapidly. Simultaneously with the feet striking the ground, the hands are pulled down in front of the face and the elbows forward of the chest to protect both the face and elbows during the landing. Study Figure 36 carefully.

REAR FALL

Assume the READY position with you back to the mat, heels slightly over the edge of the platform. On GO, jump backward and complete the fall described above.

RIGHT SIDE FALL

Assume the READY position with the right side toward the mat, right foot slightly over the edge of the platform. On GO, jump to the right and complete the fall as described above, turning the upper part of your body to the left.

LEFT SIDE FALL

Executed in the reverse manner of the right side fall.

CHECK LIST FOR PLF BODY POSITION

Face into the wind on landing.
Head erect, eyes on the horizon until moment of impact.
Feet and knees together when landing.
Make initial contact with ground on the balls of the feet.
Stay off the heels!
Drop chin to the chest and bring elbows and hands in front of chest and head upon contact with ground.
Keep body muscles tense enough to absorb the initial part of the landing shock.
Recover quickly and run around your canopy to collapse it.

COLLAPSING THE PARACHUTE

When there are no ground winds, the parachute collapses without assistance. Once landed, the jumper must be prepared to recover immediately, collapse his chute, and free himself from the parachute. This can be accomplished by one of the four methods:

Quick recovery—jump and run—method

Collapse the chute by pulling the bottom risers and suspension lines

Buddy assist method

Quick release shoulder devices

Quick Recovery: This method is generally best and quickest. To execute this, the jumper pulls either his right or left set of risers into his chest and at the same time his knees into his stomach (always executed while on back). This position tends to pivot you around in the direction of drag. When turned, kick your heels into the ground and spring to your feet and then run around the canopy to turn it against the wind.

Collapse the Chute: When you find yourself on your stomach, pull the lower risers and suspension lines into your body, hand over hand, which will allow the air to spill out over the top of your chute.

Buddy Assist: This is the method used in order to prevent damage to the chute from snags. Your buddy merely grabs the chute, preferably at the apex, and then turns it into the wind and collapses it.

Quick Release Devices: Reach up with one or both hands, release the safety catches of the shoulder releases, and then release the entire device. One release should be sufficient to allow the air to spill from your canopy.

HIGH WIND LANDINGS

Landing safely with a parachute in a high wind is not an easy task. The initial touch-down may seriously injure the jumper or knock him unconscious. The danger lies in the fact that a high wind will blow the jumper and his parachute along the ground and it is the dragging which generally causes injuries.

Since unsnapping a harness while being dragged is rather difficult, the canopy should be collapsed by pulling in on any bottom suspension lines or group of suspension lines until the canopy collapses. Since this deflating procedure can burn the hands and fingers, the lines should be grasped with a sideward twisting motion of the hands and wrists as each new snubbing grip is made along the lines. Once the canopy has been completely deflated, it is wise to sit on it while unsnapping the harness to prevent its reinflation and further dragging.

For those jumpers having canopy shoulder releases on their parachutes, merely releasing these fasteners completly frees the canopy from the jumper. All parachutists are advised to have these devices installed on their equipment for use in both high wind and water landings.

WATER LANDINGS

Fig. 37, Water Landing

There are conditions when a water landing can be safely made; however, a jumper needs to prepare himself for these in advance.

When a water landing is imminent, seat your buttocks into the saddle of the harness. Release the waistband or lower tie downs or snap fasteners of the reserve and either the right or left main snap fastener of the reserve. After insuring that you are sitting in the harness like in a swing, with no weight on the leg straps, unsnap the leg snap fasteners. If you should unsnap these fasteners while they are supporting your weight, there is great danger of falling from the harness. When nearing the water, lock your elbows down with your arms across your chest and release the chest snap fastener, (Figure 37). When your feet strike the water throw your arms aloft, arch your back, and slip out of the harness. Swim upwind and away from the parachute to avoid being entangled with it.

TREE LANDINGS

Landing in a tree is not necessarily hazardous; however, when a tree landing cannot be avoided, assume the tree landing position as shown in Figure 38 to minimize the possibility of injury during the landing. To assume this position, place your feet tightly together to protect your crotch. Place your left arm over your eyes and your left hand in your right armpit, palm outward. Place your right arm across your left arm and your right hand in the left armpit, palm outward. Turn your head slightly to the left to protect your face and throat. Maintain this position until your descent is checked. Do not attempt to grab a branch and hang on. After the descent is checked, get out of your harness. If you are suspended at a greater height than you can safely drop, release (open) your reserve parachute and slide down the suspension lines and canopy.

Fig. 38, Tree Landing

HIGH TENSION WIRE LANDINGS

Like tree landings, high tension wire landings should be avoided; however, when forced to make this type of landing, attempt to prevent your body from contacting two wires at one time, as shown in Figure 39. Place your feet together, extend your arms overhead with elbows straight, and place your hands inside and against the front risers, fingers straight. Keep your head slightly down so that you may observe and at the same time avoid coming in contact with the wires.

Fig. 39, High Tension Wire Landing

SECTION X

SAFETY, MALFUNCTIONS,
AND PHYSICAL CONDITION

Safety is the most important factor in any sport parachute jump. Every move you make and each piece of equipment used has a safety factor about it. Learn these factors well and use them. Do not rush the process of learing to be a parachutist. The reason that safety is important in parachuting is that the mistakes you make can kill you! However, if the safety rules are observed it is one of the safest sports in the nation. The fact that excellent economical insurance is available through the Parachute Club of America and that most insurance companies charge no extra premium for sport parachuting testifies to its safety.

Safety can be divided into two areas: procedures, and equipment. For example, current safety procedure calls for the jumpmaster to drop a wind drift indicator prior to each plane load of jumpers. Failure to do this constitutes a safety violation of procedure and sets up the possibility of injuring the first jumper by a landing off the drop zone. Also, on equipment safety, a physical check should be made to see that the canopy shoulder releases function properly prior to putting on the equipment. When this isn't done, and the device fails to function during a gusty landing, the possibility of a landing injury is incurred.

Actually then, in the examples above, the jumpers were not injured **by** the landing, but by setting up the injury **prior** to the jump by overlooking the safety aspects of the sport!

Like any other active sport some hazards are inherent with the game and sky diving isn't any different. However, for every hazard there is a corrective action or device which is used to compensate for or eliminate the danger.

The major hazards known to sport parachuting today are as follows:

1. Failure to pull the rip cord.
2. Being in a poor body position for opening the parachute.
3. Delaying the opening too long.
4. Going into a flat spin and holding it.
5. Jumping from over 12,000 feet without using oxygen prior to leaving the aircraft—oxygen starvation.
6. Making the long delays without proper training or after a long lay-off between jumps.

To avoid any of the above hazards, the following procedures are generally used:

1. Failure to pull rip cord. The student must make at least five good dummy rip cord pulls while on the static line parachute training to indicate to both himself and the instructor that he can and will pull the rip cord handle at the proper time. Failure to satisfactorily meet this requirement should disqualify the student from making any free falls.

2. Poor opening body position. The student learns and practices the proper body position during the initial ground training. Following this he should then stay on the static line until he can maintain control of his falling position during the fall and the dummy rip cord pull.

3. Delaying the opening to long. Students learn to count verbally so that their fall and opening can be timed. Longer falls require the use of a stopwatch and/or an altimeter which indicate the lowest point, 2500 feet, where the jumper should open the parachute. Deliberate or constant violation of this procedure should be cause for grounding the offender. The reason that the opening altitude is set for 2500 feet is so that the jumper will have an ample amount of time to use his reserve should the main canopy malfunction in some manner.

4. Flat spins. Again, correct body position should be stressed which will generally correct this condition. Students are taught to pull their rip cords immediately upon finding themselves in a flat spin. Later, when they are more proficient, the flat spins may be corrected by checking and correcting the position of the arms and feet and by using counter turns, etc.

5. Jumping from over 12,000 feet without oxygen equipment. The solution to this is to use oxygen equipment or don't jump from the higher altitudes.

6. Improper training for long delays. Students are required to start off on short delayed falls of about five seconds and gradually increase the amount of delay. Where it is

noticed that control is being lost, they should be held to this delay period until they overcome their failure and then continue to advance. When parachutists have allowed a long period of time to elapse between jumps, generally two or more months, they should be required to initially make a few short delays prior to resuming the longer delays where they left off, dependent, of course, on the ability of the individual parachutist.

To insure that safety is foremost in any club, a Club Safety Officer should be appointed to be responsible for the training, jumping, and equipment of the club, to insure that the students meet the necessary training requirements through tests, and that all procedures are safe. The safety rules of the Parachute Club of America should be used as a guide and enforced, even though your club isn't affiliated with the PCA.

In parachuting, the life you save **will** be your own!!!

MALFUNCTIONS

On very rare occassions, malfunctions may occur during some portion of your jump. These can range from a premature opening of the parachute inside the aircraft to torn fabric or a suspension line over the canopy on opening. It is toward these malfunctions that safety is stressed and that each jumper carries a reserve parachute. Actually though, a jumper can make a very poor jump, and have one or more malfunctions, and still walk away from the experience unharmed.

40 a   40 b

Fig. 40, Activating the Reserve

ACTIVATING THE RESERVE

After pulling the main parachute rip cord at 2500 feet and no opening shock is experienced within a few seconds, there is probably a malfunction. The beginner should not take the time to analyze the condition beyond the fact that the parachute is not open and that the rip cord has been pulled. After dipping either shoulder to allow

58

the pilot chute to be pulled clear of the low pressure area and there is still no opening, the chest parachute should be activated. In this case throw away the rip cord in order to free your hands for action, straighten the legs, pull the knees and feet together, and look down at your reserve parachute and reserve rip cord as shown in Figure 40. Pull the chest pack rip cord with the right hand while holding the sides of the chest pack closed with the left hand and get rid of the second rip cord. Now, letting the pack sides draw back out of the way while pressing the canopy to the pack, grasp the canopy and throw it out and away from you. The reserve should then inflate.

LINE OVER

When a suspension line flips over the canopy on opening, it might cling to the top of the inflated canopy, dividing the projected diameter to only a fraction of its original area and making the canopy resemble a large brassiere. This condition, depending on how bad it is, can greatly increase the rate of descent. If you can satisfy yourself that your rate of descent is not too great—by comparing

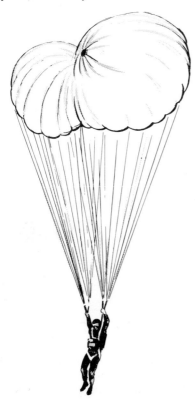

your rate to another jumper in the air or by watching the ground—time may be taken in an attempt to clear the line. To do this, grasp the line, or lines, in question and work them off the top of the canopy by pulling down on them for a short distance and then releasing them quickly. This may help to slide the lines off and reestablish the full diameter. When the lines cannot be cleared, the chest parachute should be used to supplement the loss of the main canopy's projected diameter. Prior to activating the reserve, determine the wind direction and deploy the reserve down wind which will afford a more positive and rapid inflation and reduce the chances of entangling the reserve with the open main chute. See Figure 41 for an example of a line over malfunction.

Fig. 41, Line Over

BLOWN PANEL

Fig. 42, Blown Panel

A torn parachute is not necessarily unsafe. Actually, the rate of descent can be slower due to air turbulence, caused by the air passing through the rents in the cloth, being set up over the canopy. Too many holes, or too large a hole, will add to the rate of descent. A jumper should be particularly cautious with this malfunction since the tears can become larger at any time and transform the condition into a hazardous landing. It is difficult to make any hard and fast rule regarding this malfunction, however, students will not go wrong by activating the reserve if you have many holes or large holes in the canopy. See Figure 42 for an example of the blown panel malfunction.

Fig. 43b, Cigarette Roll

Fig. 43 a & b, Cigarette Roll Occurring

CIGARETTE ROLL

A "cigarette roll" occurs when one portion of the skirt blows between two suspension lines during the opening. This causes a rapid increase in the rate of descent. Heat, generated by the friction while the nylon is being rolled up, will cause the fabric to burn and fuse and will probably weaken the panels which passed through the suspension lines. A sketch of the cigarette roll occurring is shown in Figure 43.

ACCIDENTAL OPENING OF THE RESERVE

Sometimes a student will accidentally open his reserve, particularly during the static line and dummy rip cord pull jumps. If this occurs during a static line jump, immediately gather in the reserve and hold it in to your body in any way that you can, the point being to keep it from deploying. If it does deploy along with your main canopy, your rate of descent will be about the same as normal but you will not be able to maneuver either chute effectively. Keep a careful watch on both canopies to insure that one does not foul the other.

In summary, remember that most malfunctions are caused by human error—errors in packing, errors in body position, and errors in misjudgement. However, if you are careful and seek perfection in these details, you will probably make hundreds of jumps without experiencing any major malfunctions.

PHYSICAL CONDITION

Sport parachuting requires a sensible physical condition if you want to jump frequently and continously and, at the same time, avoid injury. One doesn't require a college athlete's condition and stamina to jump; neither should one be fat and dissipated. Jumping does require the individual to be able to take the jar of landing and that muscles be used in a way that is not normal in the average day to day activities. For the routine jump a fair physical condition generally is good enough. However, it is for the abnormal jump, where a rare hard gust of wind may blow you forcefully onto the drop zone, or perhaps into an obstacle, that your physical condition will dictate whether or not you will walk away from the jump!

Any good parachute club will require that a doctor look you over and give his OK for you to make parachute jumps.

Good legs and ankles are an asset, just as they are in skiing, hiking, and most other sports. Exercises such as walking, running, bicycling, etc., can be used to good advantage in preparing the legs for jumping.

Women do not need extra equipment or safeguards since today's sport parachutes have eliminated almost all of the opening shock, and proper parachute landing fails distribute the jar of landing on the less delicate parts of the body.

Proper exercising will enable you to acquire better body positions in the air, better control in the air, and better landings. To assist you in gaining and maintaining the proper physical condition, the following exercises, all of which can be done in the home and on your own, are recommended. These should be conscientiously executed at least three times per week and before each jump session. A minimum of ten repetitions is recommended as a starting figure with the idea of increasing each exercise by a few repetitions each week.

Fig. 44, WAIST BENDER EXERCISE

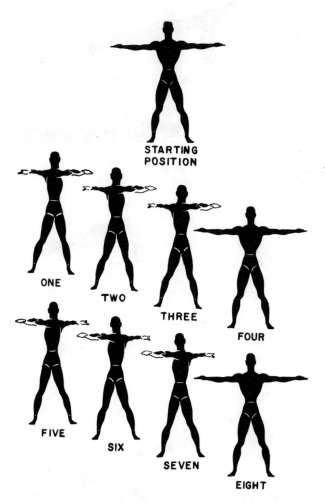

Fig. 45, Trunk Twist

PUSH UP EXERCISE

STARTING   POSITION

ONE

TWO

THREE

FOUR

Fig. 46, Push Ups

ROCK-A-BYE EXERCISE

Fig., 47, Rock-A-Bye

BACK BEND EXERCISE

STARTING
POSITION

ONE

TWO

THREE

FOUR

Fig. 48, Back Bend

ACTUAL SKY DIVER POSITION

Referring to Section VI, lie down on the floor in a relaxed manner, hands above the head and feet together. At your own signal, arch the body so that only the stomach touches the floor, spread the arms outward, raise and spread the feet and legs, and pivot the head upward. Count to five-thou-sand by thousands, which would assume a five second delay, and then relax. Have someone check this position periodically to insure that your hands, legs, and feet are equally level with their opposite member. As your body becomes more accustomed to this position, increase the time in holding the position and also make simulated rip cord pulls, holding the position for at least four seconds after the pull. Turns should also be practiced in this same manner.

PARACHUTE LANDING FALLS

These are explained in Section IX and should be practiced whenever possible, both as a method of attaining proficiency and correct physical conditioning.

GENERAL CONDITIONING NOTES

Alcohol and parachuting don't mix! Persons engaged in jumping should refrain from drinking alcoholic beverages for at least twelve hours preceding a jump and all alcohol must be restricted at the jump and packing areas. If a man or woman **needs** liquor in order to jump, then they **are** not parachutist material and should be denied the distinction. The time for liquor and jump stories is **after** the jumping has been completed and the equipment put away.

Eat lightly before and during jump sessions. You will feel better and function better. Besides, the excitement of jumping will not permit your body to properly digest any food taken during the jump period.

Get a good nights sleep prior to jump periods. An alert body and mind is needed when you are falling free at 120 miles per hour.

Students should not make more than two jumps per day. Later, after both proficiency and stamina have improved, this figure can be slowly increased. Take it easy initially. Most practical jumpers would rather be the **oldest** jumper than the one with the **most** jumps!

ON FORMING A PARACHUTE CLUB

The parachute club organizer has the task of carrying a heavy load which will occupy, if he works at it, every week-end for about the first six months! He will receive setbacks and disappointments, but, if he **really** wants to be a sky diver, and wants a parachute club or organization worthy of the name, he will overcome these difficulties somehow. A club will be only as good as the members in it! The **organizer** must make them that good.

First: Find an airfield to work out of, pilots who will fly you, and a place to jump.

2. Publicize a general request that anyone interested in sport parachuting, either as a potential jumper or a supporter, attend a general meeting to determine the interest in forming a parachute club.

3. At this meeting determine (1) if these people are just short-time thrill seekers (they won't stay with you long), (2) people who want to make only one jump or only static line jumps (they won't last either and you don't want them), or (3) people who are sincerely interested in **free-fall**, sport, and **competitive** parachute jumping who are willing to spend a good deal of their spare time in learning the sport and then, perhaps, teaching others after they have learned. The early members should be prepared to give up much of their free time and some evenings for the organization and training of themselves and the club.

This initial meeting is also the time to determine what, if any, former parachuting experience, both military and free fall, is available to start with and the most experienced and willing personnel should be asked to assit in the charter organization. It will be an asset to the club to have someone who can speak well to "sell" this new sport to all comers. For some strange reason, the phrase, "those who are not with us are against us", seems to apply to sport parachuting.

Be critically selective of your first members and the charter group. A phony can do you much harm initially. Be sure to check out the stated abilities of persons who profess to be long time free fall parachutists!

4. From the turnout at this first meeting, you should be able to determine what the future interest in the club will be, how many members the club will probably average, and what type of personnel you will have to work with. From this group a charter committee or board should be appointed to start forming the club and their missions should include at least the following items:

a. Study and learn all the provisions of the latest Parachute Club of America (PCA) Safety rules. Military clubs should also learn and understand the appropriate regulations pertaining to their particular service concerning sport parachuting.

b. Based on the above PCA safety requirements, determine where the parachutes are to come from. Many possibilities exist here such as (1) buy them from initiation dues and fees, (2) have each member purchase a share of a parachute, (3) induce local merchants or organizations to purchase and donate them to the club or even sponsor individual members, or (4) have each member purchase his own equipment from one of the many reputable dealers.

c. Determine where and what type of aircraft and qualified pilots can be obtained on a semi-permanent basis.

d. Determine the initiation fees and dues to insure that parachutes and allied equipment can be continously purchased and other expenses met. This will vary with the individual clubs due to the size of the membership body and their capacity to pay dues and fees. The lower the dues and fees, the more members the club will have.

e. Locate qualified riggers for packing, maintenance, and instruction on parachutes. If possible, obtain a club house large enough to place or build a forty foot packing table. The best location is at or near the airfield to be used.

f. Request appointment of a Safety Officer (at least a temporary one) from PCA.

g. Select a safe drop zone—A large flat area ,clear of any obstacles and as far removed from wire lines, heavily traveled roads, buildings, etc., as possible. Close-in farms are generally a good bet. After the DZ is selected, contact the local FAA representative and police officials to determine the necessary clearances to jump on your DZ.

h. Designate the personnel who will undergo the initial training under qualified instructors and who, when qualified, will become the club instructors. These initial personnel should be members who are keenly interested in sky diving and who will be available for at least six months. Men of considerable previous jumping experience, if any, should be selected.

i. Ascertain where an experienced free fall parachutist, preferably a Class B or C licensed jumper, will come from to instruct the initial group. It may be necessary to obtain one from another community in the area. The PCA and other sky diving publications can furnish you the name and address of the nearest available instructors or Safety Officers.

j. Based on the PCA requirements, plus any local guidance, write up a training and jumping program and write the individual lesson plans to be used. The guide and plans included in this book can be used for this purpose. Your final plan should be approved by the local PCA Safety Officer and the nearest FAA representative.

k. Write a club constitution and by-laws. Include the training plan as an annex as it will probably be subject to change from time to time. The constitution and by-laws should be written along the lines of the PCA Constitution and should be approved by competent legal authorities prior to adoption by the club. Advice should also be sought through legal authorities relative to insurance coverages, if any, desirable for parachute operations. The automatic insurance coverage provided by membership in the Parachute Club of America should also be investigated.

l. It will be necessary to improvise or obtain many small items such as static line anchors for various aircraft, masking tape, wind streamers, dummy rip cord handles and attachments, ananometers, parachute ground packing mats and tension devices, packing kits, stop watches, binoculars, etc., etc. A suggested list of equipment can be found at the end of this section.

5. After all of the above activities have been investigated, a workable club plan should be discussed with all supporters such as the FAA representative, airfield manager, drop zone owner, PCA representative, and various local news media. This plan should be well presented to these people by a capable interested charter member—preferably the organizer—at a time most favorable to gain their backing and support. It should be oral but should include charts, pictures, and the documents necessary to give the supporters the complete facts on which to conclude that sky diving is a safe, sane, organized sport. The basic idea behind this briefing is what a benefit this club will be to the community and to the persons participating and observing. Remember, this is a terrific spectator sport! Without support it is obvious that the club will be most difficult to organize.

6 After orientating the supporters, the first general meeting should be held. It should be widely publicized in advance and if you can get an experienced parachutist or PCA official to be a guest speaker and have him show either films or slides on sky diving, the response will surprise you. At this meeting the draft constitution should be approved, dues and fees established, members enrolled, dues and fees paid, and the permanent board of governors or club officials elected. Members nominated should be from the charter group and care should be taken in this initial election to insure that only those who will work hard for the club in their spare hours are

elected. An ineffective or lukewarm official in this stage can do much to hold back formation and training progress.

7. Initially, if possible, PCA's appointed Safety Officer should also be a member of the Club, since he will have the last word in all training and parachute jumping.

8. After the Club's formation, records **must** be accurately kept of each individual student's progress from his first orientation period to his last training free-fall. His every weakness and mistake should be noted on a form so that the Safety Officer can determine the student's ability at any time by a glance at his training record.

9. The best asset a Club can have is a good publicity agent. Have a club board member, or any qualified member, maintain a close relationship with all the local news media and keep them informed of the Club's activities. Every member should be ready to talk sky diving at the drop of a hat and drop it himself!

10. After formation, affiliation with PCA should be requested. Sky Diving, in its early stages at present, needs a common voice and PCA should be that voice. If sport parachuting is to become Olympic in stature, and it is fast on it's way now, it will only be because we banded together for the furtherance of a common goal.

11. As a final act, the following club motto should be adopted and adhered to: "Play it Safe . . . Safety First!"

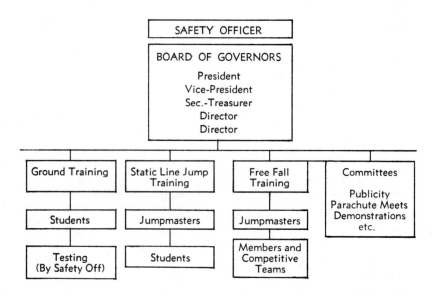

Fig. 49, Sample Organization Chart

RECOMMENDED CLUB EQUIPMENT

INDIVIDUAL EQUIPMENT:

Item:	Quantity
Football or Crash Helmet	1 per individual
Coveralls, White	1 per individual
Parachute Jump Boots	1 pair
Goggles, non-fogging type	1
Gloves, (for 32 degrees and below)	1 pair
Altimeter and/or stop watch	1, each, recommended for jumps over 8 seconds
Parachute Log Book	1
Club Insignia	1

CLUB EQUIPMENT:

Parachutes, back pack	1 per 3 members, minimum
Parachutes, chest, reserve	1 per 3 members, minimum
Packing mats, ground	3
Packing kits	3
Wind Drift Indicators (cloth)	3
Wind Drift Indicators (paper)	2 dozen
Club Parachute Log	1
Targaret Panels, white, 20x3	3
Blackboard, small	1
First Aid kit	1
Parachute kit bags	1 per chute
Shot bag weights	6
Tension Devices and hooks	3 each
Wind Anemometer	1
Binoculars	1 pair
Megaphone	1
Suspended training harness	1
Clip boards	2
Stop Watches	2

"I tole yuh I was ready for a standing landing."

GROUND AND AIR TRAINING GUIDE

Proper mental and physical conditioning is essential to insure that students are psychologically prepared and physically capable of parachute jumping with a minimum of risk of injury. Emphasis must be placed on developing the student's mental alertness and confidence in himself and his equipment.

Since most sport parachute jumping is done on the weekends, and will be in the category of recreation for many people, the training should be made as pleasant and interesting as possible. Parachuting, and the relative equipment is, in itself, interesting and it doesn't take much more than a salesman's approach to teach it to interested novices.

While one should be cautioned against going through training too fast, going too slow will discourage many would be jumpers. Certain individuals will proceed quite rapidly through the instruction and become **safe** parachutists while others may need more time to practice and learn. As a consequence, instructors should insure that everyone proceeds safely and within their own individual capabilities.

In the following outline, approximately 23 hours are spent in pre-jump ground training. This outline was used by several parachute clubs and their malfunction and injury rate, in relation to their amount of jumps, was extremely low. Other clubs may not wish to use as much time as is shown here and the outline can then be tailored to fit the needs, equipment, and members of the club.

The main point is to set up a training program which is safe! We don't even put high school boys into any sport until they have practiced, drilled, and conditioned themselves. Why should sport parachuting be different from any other sport in this respect!

So, knowing the local personnel, equipment, standards, and time that you have available for training, here is a guide which can help in organizing your own club training program.

GROUND AND AIR TRAINING PROGRAM
SECTION A: GROUND TRAINING

Period & Hours	Subject	REMARKS
Period No. 1 1 Hour	Orientation	Membership requirements, Club purposes, Training and Jumping requirements, Training Organization, PCA Safety Rules, Physical Conditioning, Main Hazards, Club Dues and Fees, Supporting Club Activities, Individual and Club Equipment, Dates, Times, and Organization of Training and Jump Periods, Question and Answer Period.
Period No. 2 1 Hour	Films, Slides, & Pictures	Period used to show films, slides, or pictures with explanations. Parachute training films are generally available on loan from service installations and slides can be taken locally to be used in briefing new students.
Period No. 3 2 Hours	Parachute Orientation	Explanation and demonstration of Blank Gore parachute from apex to leg buckles, differences between main and reserve, functioning demonstration from complete pack to inflation (on packing table or ground mat), functioning with both static line and rip cord, packing demonstration, field rolling and carrying, packing tools, care and maintenance, and fitting of parachute.
Period No. 3A 3 Hours	Parachute Packing	Evening parachute packing classes are held at the club or other area as scheduled by the instructor. No more than three students per parachute should be taught during these classes.
Period No. 4 3-5 Hours	During a jumping period rotate students between the following activities: 1. Observe and assist riggers in packing parachutes. 2. Observe and assist drop zone Safety Officer in working the DZ and observe jumpers. 3. Take observer orientation flight.	
Period No. 5 1 Hour	Aircraft Loading, Exits, and Stable Spread Positions	Aircraft Loading and seating, sequence of commands, prepare to jump positions, exit positions, stable spread position, pre-jump safety checks, spotting explanation, and pilot orientation.
Period No. 6 1½ Hours	Parachute Manipulation and Emergency Procedures	Review basic stable fall position, canopy check, counting and timing, observation of drift, slipping in four directions, turning the blank gore canopy, emergency proceedures, and dummy rip cord pulls.
Period No. 7 2 Hours	Parachute Landing Falls	Normal parachute landing falls including practical work from a PLF platform, tree, water, and high tension wire landings, recovery from drags.

| Period No. 8 | Same as Period No. 4 |
| 3-5 Hours | |

Period No. 9   Question and Answer Period for review prior to test by Safety
1 Hour   Officer.

| Period No. 10 | Performance and | Administered by the Safety Officer on all |
| 1 to 3 Hours | Written Test | training thus far received. |

NOTES:

   a.   Students passing the tests will be turned over to the jumpmaster-instructor to make first static line jump. Those failing portions of the test will be given additional training in subjects needed until the necessary proficiency is attained.

   b.   Students are generally required to observe at least one jump flight from the aircraft and one period from the ground. These can be scheduled at any time convenient during the ground training phases.

SECTION B: AIRBORNE TRAINING

Jump No.	Type	Requirement	Remarks
1	S/Line	Exit and assume Basic Stable Position, make in-air checks of parachute, ride chute to ground.	1st 7 jumps made from 2500 feet, actual. Stress position and verbal count.
2	S/Line	Same as No. 1 except executes the four directional slips and two complete turns w/blank gore parachute.	
3	S/Line	Same as No. 1 and 2 except add executes Dummy Rip Cord Pull*. Jumper must attempt to manipulate to land on target center.	*At discretion of Jumpmaster, if previous stable fall ability is proven.
4, 5, 6, & 7	S/Line	Same as No. 3. Stress target accuracy.	

NOTE: If member's last three **successive** static line jumps were satisfactory, as to both stable fall position and dummy rip cord pulls, as judged by the Jumpmaster and Safety Officer, the member will, if he so desires, be permitted to execute free falls as shown below and following a ground briefing.

| Period No. 11 | Free Fall Ground | Written jump planning, importance of counting and timing, emergency proceedures using a second count after pulling rip cord, and actions on loss of stability. |
| ½ Hour | Briefing | |

Jump No.	Type	Requirement	Remarks
FF-1	FF	Same as No. 1 w/o static line. Jump and pull w/in 5 seconds, maintain stable fall position.	No less than 2600 feet, actual, with spot landing requirement.
FF-2	FF	Same as FF-1.	
FF-3&4	Delayed Fall	Same as FF-1, except jumper may dely up to 8 seconds, maintain stable fall position.	3000 feet, actual, Spot jump.
FF-5	Delayed Fall	Same as FF-1, except jumper may delay up to 10 seconds. Maintain stable fall position.	3300 feet, actual, Spot jump.

NOTES: a. Jumpmasters may develop students slower than the schedule shown above. The delays shown are maximums which should not be exceeded.

       b. After the jumpers 5th delayed fall, jumper will be permitted to jump and delay for a period commensurate with his ability, subject to the approval of the Safety Officer. When it has been established that jumper can delay and maintain stability, turns and body maneuvering training should commence.

       c. All delays for over eight (8) seconds should require the use of either a stop watch or altimeter.

       d. After a lapse of over 30 days between free falls, the jumper should be required to make only a 5 second delay on his next jump.

       e. After a lapse of over 60 days between free falls, the jumper should be required to make a static line dummy rip cord pull on his next jump, followed by a 5 second delay free fall.

SECTION C: ADVANCED TRAINING

Period No. 12 Jumpmaster   Techniques of jumpmastering, preparation
1 Hour   Training   of aircraft, pilot briefing, loading zone and
                                  drop zone operation, Safety Checks, written
                                  jump planning, training records, and brief-
                                  ing students

Period No. 13 Basic Turns, Door Exits.
1 Hour

SECTION XIII

"How do I read my instruments?"

INDIVIDUAL SUBJECT TEACHING GUIDES

The following general subject teaching guides were prepared for use by instructors in teaching the basic elements of sport parachuting. There is one guide for each period of instruction shown in the preceding section and they are presented here in the same order. It is recommended that the same sequence be used regardless of other changes you may wish to make in the program.

A test has been omitted since each club will probably wish to make up their own program based on the methods of instruction used.

PERIOD 1

Subject: **Orientation**
Time: 1 Hour
Training Aids Required: Charts: Stable Fall Positions; Photos of Jumping Activities.
Area Required: Classroom

ORIENTATION

Introduce self
Assumption: That everyone here is interested in Sport Parachuting.

Today, a few Americans are struggling to awaken the interest of other Americans in a sport that is positively the greatest sport challenge to both individual men and teams of men ever to arrive on our national sport scene; a sport of skill, strength, daring, stamina, and "guts" . . . Sport Parachuting!

Now just **what** is this new Sky Diving? It's a sport in which a man **exits** himself from an aircraft at high altitude, **stabilizes** himself in free fall, **changes** direction at will or on signals, **executes** precision turning, diving, rolls, and baton-passing body maneuvers at prescribed times and altitudes, **doesn't lose** control during fall, **opens his parachute** at a prescribed altitude, place and time, and then **manipulates** his parachute so as to land on the center of a given target. During competition he is graded on each of these requirements as to **form, proficiency, timing,** and **accuracy.**

PURPOSES OF CLUB:

1. Provide an opportunity for interested persons to engage in sky diving parachute jumping.
2. Promote interest in sport parachuting.
3. Further competitive sport relationships between clubs, school, cities, states, and countries.
4. Provide an opportunity for parachutists to maintain their proficiency.
5. Furnish parachute jumpers to compete in local, national, and international competition.
6. Teach sport parachuting to persons who desire to learn.

What must you do to become a jumping member:

1. Apply for club and PCA membership, be accepted by the Club officers and pay your dues.
2. Complete the necessary physical examination.
3. Complete the pre-jump ground training and pass the exams.
4. Be in physical condition to make parachute jumps.
5. Make the necessary training static line jumps.

TRAINING

a. a. **Long range training program:** First to . . . train everyone in 5 to 15 second free fall parachute jumps and to hold a stabilized falling position in the air, Second, to proceed into accuracy in spot jumping, longer delayed free falls (16-60 seconds), and, simultaneously, actual Sky Diving or body manipulation during free fall, according to international competition requirements.

b. **Priority of training:**
1. Complete pre-jumping ground training.
2. Complete static line jumps fullfilling the basic stable fall position requirements.
3. Complete static line jumps fullfilling the basic stable fall position **and** dummy rip cord pull requirements.
4. Complete free falls, increasing delays up to 30 seconds.
5. Complete free falls, increasing delays up to 60 seconds.

TRAINING ORGANIZATION

a. Train one class per month starting 1st Saturday of each new month.
b. Training commences each Saturday at.............................
c. Parachute jumping on both Saturday and Sundays.
d. Instructors selected by their experience and ability. These instructors will give the ground training. (Introduce this class' instructor(s).
e. Training broken down as follows:
(1) 1 Hour Club orientation.
(2) 1½ hours training films or slides.
(3) 1 hour—Parachute orientation.
(4) 3 hours—Method of Exit.
(5) 1½ hours—Parachute Maneuvering and Emergency Procedures.
(6) 3 hours—Parachute Landing.
(7) Various hours—Observation of jumping, both from Drop Zone and in aircraft.
(8) Parachute packing.
(9) Testing.
(10) Static Line jumps.
(11) Free Fall jumps.
(12) Jumpmaster Training.

The Big Question . . . When can I jump?

Previously qualified military parachutists: take the necessary free fall training subjects, prove to the instructors concerned that you know how, pass the tests, and when the Safety Officer clears you to jump.

Novices: On successful completion of the pre-jump ground training, pass the test, and after the Safety Officer clears you to jump, based on your training performance and attitude.

Any Questions on Training?

Importance of Club Training: The mistake that you make may kill you. We here are the initial pioneers. It is on our conduct and records that this sport will either flourish or be abolished.

SAFETY: The Club watchword is **safety.**

(Read)   "It is far more important that SAFETY rules be observed than to rush someone into the sport of parachuting and risk even one fatality!! If there should be a single death or serious injury from **carelessness,** or non-observance of training and safety regulations, it could kill the sport and nullify the long work that has gone into the program thus far."

The above should be your club motto.

Because you may have been a military parachutist, don't be fooled into thinking that you can be a **SAFE** sky-diver over-night.

(Ask free-fallers present their opinion of going slow.)

Some members will say that we're too restrictive . . . Or that our program is to basic for seasoned ex-military jumpers.

To these we ask patience . . . and practice, for it's in **their** safety we are interested. Too often the first training for a novice has been a free fall jump . . . and in some cases this was also the last training. We don't want **any** injuries or fatalities in this club . . . ever!!

Physical Conditioning

Along with Safety goes your physical conditioning.

No formal PT program here, PT is the members own responsibility. If you don't appear to be in shape to the Jumpmaster, no jumping.

In your training for exits from aircraft you will be shown some exercises which will assist in keeping you fit for jumping and develop the necessary arch and spread. These should be done frequently as long as you intend to be a jumper.

The opposite of Safety is HAZARD:

. . . and right now, early in the game, I'd like to make you familiar with what we consider the four main hazards in free-fall parchute jumping: (Write these down.)

1. Failure to pull the rip cord (80% of accidents from this)
2. Improper body position for parachute opening
3. Going into "flat spin" during the free-fall phase (250 rpm . . . causing blackout and death)
4. Delaying the opening too long

Explain each one and enumerate how we teach to eliminate these:

1. Dummy Rip-cord pulls and holding position.
2. Stable Fall position requirements.
3. Pull on initial spin, later use body correction and extreme arch.
4. Use count, stop watch, and altimeters.

Any Questions so far?

As I said earlier, this Parachute Club is new and it needs members to get it going and keep it going; however, this club is only going to be as good as the members in it!

To be a good member will take some of your spare time and effort, not just to complete the training and jumping, but to be an active, participating member. It's **your** club. Much has already been done for you (mention items) but now we want everyone to pitch-in and keep it going.

The first matter along this line is: **Paying your dues promptly.**

Policy on dropping for non-payment of dues. If you cannot support your club, it cannot support your jumping, simple!

The second matter is: **Supporting the club for necessary details.**

These will be few and spread thin so they shouldn't work any hardship on anyone.

For one Jumping Session we will need: (Read LZ and DZ requirement list). We normally ask for volunteers for these periods and if this works, no problem. However, if not, we have to detail members to get the job done. Please remember, that when you are jumping it will take the same number of details as when others jump.

Individual Equipment

Members should get all their jumping equipment as soon as they become members.

78

Reasons: Check it out
Good publicity
Need it anyway later on
Keep your other clothes clean
You may purchase and use your own parachute **after they have
been cleared** through the Rigger and Safety Officer.

Club Equipment

New parachutes cost up to $350.00 each, reserves, $175.00.

Many men have gone to great lengths to make us many items which are costly to replace. Take care of this equipment or we will be a parachute club without parachutes. Pay particular attention to this maintenance factor in your parachute orientation and packing classes.

Club Policies: (enumerate)

No dues . . . no jump. Publicity and announcements: Read Club Bulletin Board.

Any Questions? Turn group over to Instructor.

After you see the Secretary, we'll start the next period: **Training Films, Slides, or Pictures.**

PERIOD 2

SUBJECT: **Training Films, Slides, or Pictures.**
TIME: 1½ Hours
TRAINING AIDS REQUIRED   1   16mm Projector and Speaker,
                                              Films, Slides
                                     1   Screen
                                                Photographs
AREA REQUIRED: (Club Room, Darkened)

1. Introduction:

During the next 1½ hours you will see some training films on how to do certain functions in connection with parachute jumping. These are military films used for training military parachutists; however, they are excellent for sport parachutists and, with some exceptions which will be explained to you after each film, portray exactly how we want you to perform while learning parachuting.

2. Show Training Films. (These US Army films may be borrowed from most any Army installation.)

1st Film: TF 10-2455 (17 min) **Emergency Parachute Jumps**
Comments **after** film:
Disregard the method of rolling up parachute after landing.
Questions?

2d Film: TF 31-2128 **Personnel Parachute Malfunctions and Activation of Reserve.**
Comments **after** film:
We don't use pilot chute in our reserves.
Briefly review our reserve procedures.
Questions?

3d Film: TF 31-2129 **Entanglements and Recovery From Twists**
Questions?

4th Film: TF 31-2130 **Parachute Landing Falls**
Questions?

(If films are not available, use slides or photos)

3. Summary

Remember what you have seen here today. You will see these things again on the test and, more important, you may see some of the malfunctions in the air. It will be at this time that you must know what to do, when to do it, and how!
Questions?

PERIOD 3

SUBJECT: **Parachute Orientation, Packing, and Fitting**
TIME: Two (2) hours; Instruction and Practical Work
TRAINING AIDS REQUIRED: 1.   Blank Gore and Reserve Parachute
                                       2.   Assistant instructor in complete jump uniform
                                       3.   Packing equipment
                                       4.   Diagram of parachute and sleeve functioning
AREA: Indoor Packing Table or Outdoor Ground Mat

I. INTRODUCTION

1. The purpose of this instruction is to familiarize the student with the parachute and the procedure necessary to insure safe packing and handling.
2. This training is necessary to familiarize the student with the nomenclature and functioning of the parachute.

II. EXPLANATION

1. Nomenclature: point out the following parts and explain their function
   a. Main lift web
   b. Rip-cord pocket and housing
   c. Rip-cord
   d. Capewell Releases
   e. Quick release chest fastener
   f. "D" Ring
   g. Reserve parachute
      (1) Rip-cord handle
      (2) Pins and cones
      (3) Flap
      (4) Quick opening bands
   h. Leg straps and quick releases
   i. Adjustment straps
   j. Reserve adjustment, lower tie down or snaps
   k. Blank Gore back pack
      (1) 28 ft. canopy
      (2) Pack tray or container
      (3) Static line and retainer ring
      (4) Risers
      (5) Protective flap
      (6) Opening bands
      (7) Rip-cord pins and cones
2. Functioning: demonstrate and explain functioning cycle
   a. Activation of rip-cord or static line
   b. Action of quick opening bands
   c. Pilot chute
   d. Bridal loop and connecting line w/stowage
   e. Sleeve
   f. Stowage and sleeve flap
   g. Suspension lines
   h. Canopy
      (1) Gores and panels
      (2) Blank gore
      (3) Breather
      (4) Skirt
   i. Risers and connector links
   j. Back pack

III. REVIEW

1. Stress six (6) main parts of chute
   a. Pilot chute
   b. Sleeve
   c. Canopy
   d. Suspension lines
   e. Harness
   f. Pack tray
2. Stress safety requirements
   a. Never leave chute when packing
   b. Chutes packed or repacked every sixty (60) days
   c. No smoking while packing or in vicinity of chutes
3. Cover material to be presented in practical work packing classes
4. Schedule group night packing classes

IV. APPLICATION (To be accomplished at Night packing sessions during ground training—Period 3A)

1. Demonstrate packing of one complete BLANK GORE
   a. Cover nomenclature again
   b. Correct packing procedure
   c. Re-emphasize care and maintenance of parachute and equipment
   d. Point out packing tools and their role

      (1) Tension device
      (2) Fingers
      (3) Shot bags
      (4) Spreaders and pilot chute alignment pipe
      (5) Pack paddles
      (6) Rubber retaining bands
2. Practical exercise by students: Instructor should insure that all students are working on one phase or another during the whole training period.
  a. Prepare chute for packing
  b. Flaking
  c. Compressing pilot chute
  d. Stowage of connecting line
  e. Placing canopy in sleeve
  f. Stowing of suspension lines
  g. Packing
  h. Fitting of main and reserve
     (1) Review nomenclature
     (2) Stress capewell release for emergency
3. Instructors will maintain records of individual weaknesses in packing. When instructor feels that student is ready for packing test, it will be scheduled. During the test no corrections will be made. After chute is completely packed, the instructor will check the packing, critique the student, and recommend him for additional training, if necessary.

V. SUMMARY
Student should be constantly reminded of safety regulations in packing, i.e, when chutes should be repacked, specific points to look for in packing, such as correct stowage of suspension lines and connecting line.

PERIOD 3A

SUBJECT: **Parachute Packing Practice**
TIME: 3 Hours
TRAINING AIDS: 3 Blank Gore Parachutes, Complete
                 3 Packing Tables or mats
                 1 Riggers Kit, Complete
                 1 Functioning Chart
                 1 Packing Sequence Chart
                 1 Parachute Nomenclature Chart
                 2 Asst Instructors
AREA: Indoor or Outdoor Packing Area (Indoor preferred)
1. At the present time only qualified riggers are authorized to pack a parachute. However, It is necessary to learn to pack the parachute to:
  a. Understand the functioning.
  b. Build your confidence in the chute itself.
  c. Learn the nomenclature so as to talk intelligently and report the functioning or malfunctioning.
  d. Assist the riggers in repacking.
  e. Teach others after you become proficient at packing.
2. Explanation of Nomenclature, Functioning, and Packing Sequence Using Charts.
3. Practical Work.
  a. Group is broken into three groups.
     (1) Group 1: Flakes and Inspects Parachute on Packing Table or Mat, Puts on Sleeve, Stows Sleeve Retainer Line.
     (2) Group 2: Stows Suspension lines and folds Parachute, prepares pilot chutes,
     (3) Group 3: Closes Parachute Pack with both Rip Cord and Static Line, Stows Static Line, Inspects Parachute for pre-jump Safety Check. Fits parachute to self.
4. Question—Answer Period
5. Summary
  a. Remember, whenever you pack a parachute, you should be willing to jump it. If you are not willing to jump it, then repack it!
  b. Always take care of your chute properly. Keep it dry, clean, and away from all grease and acids. Treat the Club's 'chutes as if they were your own . . . since it actually will be your own when you pull the rip cord. Report any violations of care and maintenance to the Safety Officer. Report even the most minor discrepancies to the Rigger—make sure before proceeding!
6. Clean up packing area and stow gear.

PERIOD 4

SUBJECT: **Student Observation of Jumps, Assisting in Parachute Repack, and Assisting on the Drop Zone.**
TIME: 3 to 5 Hours
TRAINING AIDS: None
AREA: Loading Zone and Drop Zone
1. **Introduction**
   Today you are going to work in three groups: Loading Zone, Drop Zone, and Aerial Observer.
2. **Operation:**
   a. **Loading Zone:** Those in the loading—repack zone will assist the riggers in repacking 'chutes, getting other jumpers ready to jump, and observing the activities in this area. Be careful of the parachutes and of the packing equipment. Observe the Jumpmaster's Safety check of each parachutist prior to enplaning.
   b. **Drop Zone:** Those on the Drop Zone will observe the jumps, assist the Drop Zone Safety Officer as he directs, assist in collapsing the jumpers 'chute when necessary, help roll-up 'chutes and carry jump gear off the DZ, observe how the DZ is set up, learn the operation of the anamometer, and study the panel signals.
   c. **Air Observers:** The aerial observers will load in the aircraft as directed and observe all procedures used in jumping a planeload. Watch each jumper and critique each man as to exit, fall, and opening. (Jumpmasters should observe student-observers in the air to detect nervousness, attitude, etc.)
3. Although you may not be rotated through all three duties today, you will complete the cycle prior to your own jumps.
4. At the completion of the jump period, assist whatever group you are with in assemblying, checking, and bringing in the Club equipment.
5. **Summary**
   Have a question-answer period after students have assembled. If they have no questions, ask questions to see what students learned during period.

PERIOD 5

SUBJECT: **Aircraft Exits, Stable Spread Position, Jump Techniques**
TIME: 1 hour
TRAINING AIDS: Charts: Aircraft Exits
                Stable Fall Positions
                Jump Commands (Hand Signals)
                Body Position Check
        Main and Reserve Parachute
        1 Ass't Instructor and demonstrator
        1 Aircraft (Type from which jumps will be made)
        Wind Indicator
        Dummy Rip-cord
AREA: Airstrip
1. **Introduction**
   a. Purpose of Instruction: To teach pre-jump and jump techniques, to include conduct in the aircraft and proper exits. All pointed toward future free-fall jumping. Class will include both lecture and practical work.
   b. Breakdown of instruction:
   (1) Pre-jump Safety Check by individual and Jump-master
   (2) Pilot Orientation
   (3) Emergency Procedures
   (4) Aircraft Loading and Seating
   (5) Spotting and Use of Wind Indicator
   (6) Pre-jump Commands
   (7) Jump Technique, including Position and Stable Spread
2. **Lesson Outline**
   a. **Pre-Jump Safety Check** (use a demonstrator, completely rigged)
   (1) Clothing
       (a) Helmet: Snug fit, Chin Strap snug and securely fastened
       (b) Goggles: Snug fit, fit properly within helmet space, clean.
       (c) Coveralls: Sleeves free of hands, collar tucked down.
       (d) Parachute Boots: Securely laced, proper type and supporting ankles.

(2) Equipment
  (a) Parachute:
    (1) Back: Rip Cord Cover Snapped, opening bands all there, Nylon not showing.
    (2) Static Line: Static line properly stowed. Snap fastener in order; test. (over correct shoulder).
    (3) Harness: Rip Cord handle attached to cable and in recess. Harness straps complete, w/o twists. Frayed or worn webbing. "D" and/or "V" rings in order. Capewell releases fastened.
    (4) Harness fitting: Snug, evenly distributed. Excessively long straps taped down. Buckles and snap fasteners correct position on body. Rip Cord handle unobstructed. (Dummy Rip Cord handle, when applicable.) Riser connections centered on body harness.
  (b) Reserve: Fastened on "D" rings properly.
      Locking pins in order.
      Front Flap snapped.
      Rip Cord on right side.
      No silk showing.
      Frayed or damaged cloth.
      Elastic opening bands secure and present.
      Lower tie downs or snap fasteners secure.
      Right carrying handle tied down secure.
  (c) Altimeter, stop watch, knife, secure
  (d) Kit Bag: Under chest fastener and reserve. (if any)

Jumpmaster—
 b. **Pilot Orientation** (Mention only in passing)
    (1) Characteristics of the aircraft
    (2) Setting the altimeter
    (3) Problems for pilot in dropping parachutists
    (4) Pilot-Jumpmaster co-ordination
    (5) Jumper hazards to and conduct in aircraft
    (6) Speed in flying, approach, and over exit point
    (7) Communication (Panels)
 c. **Emergency Procedures**
    (1) Instructions from Pilot prior to take-off . . . Obey these!
    (2) Seat belts—take off and landing
    (3) For Static Line jumpers:
        Exit on Pilot/Jumpmaster order. Without hooking-up; pull reserve on clearing aircraft. Jumpmaster will jetison all doors and issue order to jump. Jumpmaster will exit behind last jumper.
    (4) For Free-falls: Same as above
        Note: Under 500 feet all persons remain in aircraft, fasten seat-belts; and prepare to make forced landing.
    (5) Smoking Rules
 d. **Aircraft Loading and Seating:**
    (1) Load only on Jumpmaster's instructions.
    (2) Order of loading: (Demonstrate with Ass't Instructor as Jumpmaster and 3 students)
        Load in reverse order of jump. Seats designated by Pilot/JM
    (3) Once aircraft has started to move, no personnel will change their positions except on command of the Jumpmaster or pilot.
 e. **Spotting Technique** (Mention in passing)
    (1) Explanation of procedures (Blackboard)
    (2) Dropping of wind indicators (Only Jumpmaster will drop)
    (3) Panel Signals—learn these (Chart)
 f. **Prepare to Jump** (Explain and Demonstrate)
    (1) **Aircraft Hand Signals:**
        (a) Are you ready? (Hand raised, palm toward jumper)
        (b) Move to "prepare to jump" position. (Thumb movement toward open door (and hook-up motion if Static Line is used)
        (c) Position. (Point to ground several times)
        (d) Go. (Firm slap on butt or leg)
 g. **Go:** (Explain and Demonstrate Stable Spread Position)
    (1) **Action:** Jumper will throw both feet rearward and upward, parallel to the flight of the aircraft, and then push rearward with both arms. He will in-

stantly spread both legs and raise both arms away from his sides in a spread-eagle fashion, body arched, head thrown back, eyes on the horizon.
   (2) **Position Check:** (Chart—Basic Stable Fall Position)
      (a) Head: Back with eyes on the horizon.
      (b) Chest: Raised and arched.
      (c) Arms: Spread wide at right angles to body, hands relaxed, fingers open. Both arms at same angle and same height.
      (d) Back: Arched as much as the conformation of the body will allow— Strain!
      (e) Legs: Spread wide apart, equally level, knees straight without stiffness.
   (3) **Count**
   (4) **Rip-Cord Pull**
3. **Practical Work:**
  a. Physical Exercises
   (1) Side-Straddle-hop, stretch and arch
     (First done standing, then on ground)
   (2) Stretch and arch, Dummy Rip-cord Pulls
     (First done standing, then on ground)
  b. Dry Runs; practical work on Exits from Aircrafts
  c. Dry Runs; loading, seating, commands, and exiting aircraft
4. **Summary of Instruction**
  a. Check your equipment before putting it on (**Your Responsibility**)
  b. Once aboard aircraft, take all instructions from Jumpmaster.
  c. Practice the stable-spread position and arch every time you can.
  d. Practice your emergency pull procedures whenever possible. Think!
  e. A reminder that good physical condition may mean the difference between a good stable position and a poor one and a good landing and an injurious one.
5. **Question-Answer Period**
6. Replace aircraft equipment, assemble and check Club gear, clean up area.

PERIOD 6

SUBJECT: **Parachute Manipulation, Emergency Procedures, and Preparing to Land.**
Time: 1½ Hours
TRAINING AIDS: Charts: Stable Fall Position
               Canopy Gore Turning Diagram
               Mid-air Check Sequence
         Suspended Harness Mock Up
        1 Asst Instructor and Demonstrator
AREA: Harness Mock-Up Area
ORGANIZATION FOR INSTRUCTION: A 90 minute class, ten minutes of which will be devoted to review of the stabilized fall position and count, thirty minutes to an explanation and demonstration of parachute maneuvering, and fifty minutes of practical work in parachute maneuvering.
1. Introduction: During this instruction we will take up methods of maneuvering the parachute in the air.
   Reasons: 1. To enable jumper to hit designated target.
         2. To avoid injury.
         3. Points may be gained in competition by proper maneuvering of the parchute during spot jumping.
         4. Avoid collision with both ground and aerial obstructions.
2. Explanation and Demonstration:
  A. Review of stabilized fall position and count.
    1. Stabilized fall position—Face to earth, arms extended in plane of body slightly below shoulders, palms to earth, fingers extended and spread apart, legs level with body and spread apart.
    2. Count: Count commences immediately upon leaving aircraft. On static line jumps, it terminates with opening of parachute. On free falls first count series terminates with activation rip cord. Second count series commences with rip cord activation and terminates with parachute opening. Remember, the tendency is to count **too fast!!!**
  B. Procedure on opening of parachute.
    1. Clear twists.

2. Check canopy to see that it is fully inflated and for malfunctions.
   a. Mae West
   b. Blown panels
   c. Cigarette Roll
3. Look for Target.
4. Face into the wind.
5. Check drift.
6. Manipulate knobs—Right knob for right turn, left knob for left turn.

C. Guidance of parachute in the air.
   1. Aerodynamic characteristics of open gore parachute.
      a. Escape of air through open gore causes 6-8 mph motion by parachute away from open gore.
      b. Air thru vent cuts down oscillation.
   2. Slipping procedures (Explain how air slips out from under canopy.)
      a. Right slip
      b. Left slip
      c. Front slip
      d. Back slip
      e. Diagonals
      f. Right and left turns using turning devices
   3. Determination of drift direction (Look over feet and determine drift direction).
      a. Drift direction resultant of wind direction—slipping procedures and use open gore to assist in maneuvering.
   4. Demonstration of slipping procedures.

D. Preparing to land.
   Prepare to land when approximately 50 ft. from ground.
   Prepare to land position: Eyes straight to front, arms extended overhead grasping high up on risers, legs together, knees slightly bent, toes pointed downward, body relaxed.

E. Emergency procedures.
   1. Possible malfunctions:
      a. Loss of lifting surface (Blown Panels)
      b. Failure to deploy (vacuum over back)
      c. Failure to inflate (Streamer)
      d. Complete malfunction
   2. Action on directing malfunction:
      a. Emergency body position—Feet and legs together, hands on reserve parachute, right hand on rip cord, chin tucked in.
      b. Activation: Strong pulling motion of reserve rip cord and drop away, feeding out of parachute and inflation by shaking out if necessary. (No pilot chute.)
      c. When in doubt—Pull!

F. Review of previous instruction.
   Practical Exercise: Students will don harness for practical work:
   1. Parachute maneuvering—slips and turns.
   2. Emergency procedures—body positions and pull.
   3. Prepare to land—body position.

PERIOD 7

SUBJECT: **Parachute Landing Falls**
TIME: 2 Hours
TRAINING AIDS: 3 foot high platforms on soft ground or mat, Drag harness
AREA: Outdoors (on soft ground or mat)

1. Introduction
   During this period you will learn one of the most important acts in parachute jumping—landings. A good landing is one that you can walk away from! Each landing must be done right on the first try and you have only a fraction of a second to do it correctly. In this area you should strive for perfection.
   We will use only the military PLF. Students will not try to make standing landings until cleared by the Safety Officer. (Generally after at least 25 jumps)

2. Lesson Outline.
   a. Explanation and demonstration of Front PLF:

(1) The student takes his place on the platform. He then receives the command of "Ready" At this time he raises his arms over his head, hands closed into a fist, knuckles to the front. His toes, knees, and heels together, knees slightly bent, eyes on the horizon. On the command "Go" he jumps up and out, clearing the platform. Once his toes touch the ground, he pulls his elbows into his chest and his fists over his face, (to protect the face and chest). Remember, your toes and knees are together through the Landing. The jumper turns his body so his calf hits the ground and then allows the shock to be absorbed by his thigh, buttocks, and push-up muscles. The shock is taken up by the Five Points of Contact, almost simultaneously.

(2) Check points:

    (a) Toes and knees together.

    (b) Knees and upper part of the body turn in either direction of fall in a front PLF.

    (c) Points of Contact:

        Balls of feet (emphasis—stay off heels).

        Calf of the leg.

        Thigh.

        Buttocks

        Push-up muscles in back.

(3) Four Types of Parachute Landing Falls:

    Front . . Rear . . . Right . . . left.

    (a) Demonstrate each fall . . . By-the-numbers.

(4) **Practical Work:** Students line up to the jump platform, mount on the instructor's order, obtain the prepare to jump position, and jump off, executing the landing fall called for by the instructor. Be sure men recover quickly. Instructor grades each student PLF

b. **Landing Recovery From Drag** (Explain circumstances)

(1) Once landed, the jumper must be prepared to recover immediately, collapse his chute, and free himself from the parachute. This can be accomplished by one of four methods:

    Quick recovery—"jump and run" (Empasize).

    Collapse the chute by pulling the bottom riser and suspension lines.

    Buddy Assist

    Quick Release

(2) **Quick Recovery:** This method is best and quickest. To do this the jumper pulls either his right or left set of risers into his chest and at the same time his knees into his stomach. (Always executed while on back.) This position tends to pivot you around in the direction of drag. When turned, kick your heels into the ground and spring to your feet.

(3) **Collaspe the Chute:** When you find yourself on your stomach, pull the lower risers and suspension lines into your body, hand over hand, which will allow the air to spill out over the top of your chute.

(4) **Buddy Assist:** This is the method used in order to prevent damage to the chute from snags. Your buddy merely grabs the chute and collapses it.

(5) **Quick Release:** Reach up and release the Capewell shoulder releases. One release should be sufficient to allow the air to spill from under canopy.

c. Explain and demonstrate the following landings:

(1) Water—emphasize the early clearing of harness.

(2) Tree—protection.

(3) High-tension wire.

    Have students execute these landing positions.

d. Question-Answer period.

3. **Summary**

Emphasize that good physical condition is necessary to make good landings. Practice daily and continue to practice.

4. Clean up area and secure Club equipment.

Be sure students are graded on their PLF performance.

PERIOD 10

SUBJECT: **Conduct of Test**
TIME: 3 Hours
TESTING AIDS: PLF Platform
             Aircraft rigged for exits
             Suspended Harness
AREA: Performance Test—Outdoor Training area and Air Strip
       Written Test—Classroom

1. Introduction
   During the next three hours you will be put thru all the phases of training thus far given to determine if you have learned well enough to start jump training. If you do well you will be turned over to a Jumpmaster as soon as you can be scheduled into a flight. For those who fail, additional training will be given until the desired proficiency is attained.
2. Breakdown of Testing:
   Performance Test—
       (1) Aircraft exits—Three good exits in a row including position, count, arch.
       (2) PLF's: Three good PLF's of Front, Rear, and Right or Left.
       (3) Slips and Turns: Demonstrate correct slips and turns called for by the Instructor.
       (4) Landings: Demonstrate prepare to land positions as called for by the Instructor.
       (5) Emergency Procedure: Demonstrate Emergency Procedure as called for by the Instructor.
   Written Test: (1 hour allowed)
       (1) Students move to classroom area and take written test. After papers are turned in, Instructor will go over test, one question at a time, giving correct answers.
3. At completion of testing notify students who have and have not passed the performance test. Grade written test as soon as possible and post results on club bulletin board. Instruct those not passing on what they must continue training· in prior to retesting.
4. Assemble testing gear and return to Club.

PERIOD 11

SUBJECT: **Pre-Jump Free Fall Briefing**
Time: 30 Minutes
TRAINING AIDS: Chart—4 main Hazards
                 Altimeter and Stop Watch Plate
                 Delay Computation Chart (or PCA Log Book)

1. Introduction
   Purpose of briefing is to clear up any doubts that you may have relative to free falls. Procedures as to safety checks, loading, exits, and stable position are the same. Only difference is that you will delay 5 seconds after leaving aircraft and then open your own parachute.
2. Orientation:
       a. Computation of jump altitude from chart.
       b. Timing-counting and use of stop watch.
       c. Written planning of entire jump to include:
           (1) Selecting length of delay
           (2) Computing time for delay
           (3) Planning free fall maneuvers
           (4) Selecting opening point
       d. Stress Arch and Count
       e. What to do if you:
           (1) Go out of control—vigorous arch and hold
           (2) Flat Spin-arch and pull
           (3) Nose Dive-arch hard and pull (head back)
           (4) Roll-Arch and spread
           (5) Don't feel main open after pull and count of four thousand—dip either shoulder slightly. If no opening then, pull reserve.
       f. Loss of Control Causes:
           (1) Flat Spin: Legs or arms not level, body twisted
           (2) Dive: arms rearward, shoulders hunched.
           (3) Roll: Arms, legs—sudden arm, leg movement

(4) Tumble: Loss of arch
(5) Buffeting: Arms forward
g. Don't kick feet and legs to recover-arch!
3. Question-Ansewer Period.

PERIOD 12

SUBJECT: **Jumpmaster Training**
TIME: One (1) Hour
REFERENCES: 1. PCA Regulations
              2. Club Safety Rules
              3. Club Training Program
TRAINING AIDS REQUIRED 1. Complete main and reserve.
                              2. Jumpmaster equipment checklist.
                              3. Wooden cutouts for spotting technique.
                              4. Evaluation forms.
                              5. Sketch or aerial photograph of DZ.
                              6. One Assistant Instructor.
AREA: Classroom.
I. Introduction.
  1. Necessity of training is to qualify all members for the job of Jumpmaster and Drop Zone Controller.
  2. Outline of instruction:
    a. Classroom instruction.
    b. Practical work in aircraft.
      (1) Assistant Jumpmaster.
      (2) Jumpmaster.
II. Techniques of Jumpmastering:
  1. Preparation of aircraft; varies with aircraft used.
    a. Placement of platform for exiting.
    b. Tape all sharp edges.
    c. Tape impact area of static lines.
    d. Check aircraft altimeter.
    e. Check aircraft commo.
  2. Preparation of manifest if required by pilot.
  3. Brief Pilot.
    a. Location of DZ; (use aerial photograph or sketch).
    b. Drop speed of aircraft.
    c. Number of jumpers.
    d. Number of passes.
    e. Altitude for each pass.
    f. Method of turning so wind streamer, jumper, and ground signals are observed.
    g. Emergency procedures.
  4. Jumpmaster equipment checklist: (mimeograph copy to each student).
    a. Helmet and glasses secure.
    b. No twists in harness and risers.
    c. Capewells closed and secured.
    d. Chest snap secure.
    e. Reserve rings fastened securely.
    f. Check pins in reserve.
    g. Check quick opening bands on reserve.
    h. Check lower tie downs on reserve.
    i. Quick releases on leg straps secured.
    j. Leg straps straight
    k. Static line not tangled or twisted, correct stow.
    l. Pins straight in cones and backed out slightly.
    m. Quick opening bands secured.
    n. Side adjustment straps knotted.
  5. Instructions to jumpers: utilize planning jump sheet.
    a. Know what jump each jumper is making.
    b. Tell students what they will do.
    c. Go over planned jump with each free faller.
  6. Conduct in aircraft.
    a. Commo w/pilot.
    b. Streamer from 2200 ft. actual.

c. Method of spotting.
   (1) Visual measurement.
   (2) Counting and stop watch method.
d. Static line drops from 2500 ft. actual.
e. Free falls.
7. Utilization of assistant jumpmaster (larger aircraft).
  a. Preparation of aircraft.
  b. Manifest.
  c. Equipment check.
  d. Instructions to jumpers.
  e. Assist in exiting static line jumpers.
   (1) Hook up static line.
   (2) Observe exiting.
  f. Observe streamers.
8. Jump commands and signals.
  a. Ready.
  b. Move to door position (and hook up).
  c. Board or exit position.
  d. Jump and/or GO!
9. Jumpmaster responsible for posting jump record and debriefing of students on ground.
  a. Record performance of each jumper; weaknesses and strong points.
  b. Number of seconds on delays.
  c. Information to be written immediately after jumper exits aircraft and turned over to records secretary for posting to student's training records.
10. Always stress safety!

DROP ZONE CHECK LIST

I. Check-list: Following equipment required on DZ:
  1. Anamometer.
  2. Target and signal panels.
  3. Stretcher and First Aid Kit.
  4. Parachute kit bags.
  5. Grading forms.
  6. Sufficient transportation.
  7. Stop-watch and field glasses.
  8. Smoke signals, if available.

II. Instructions:
  1. Know your ground-to-air signals.
   a. X   DROP OK; wind not exceeding 8 mph steady.
   b. I   NO DROP—Land aircraft.
   c. T   NO DROP, MAKE ANOTHER PASS WITH AIRCRAFT.
   d. Y   (Experienced jumpers only; wind between 10-15 mph.
  2. Know how to read anamometer! Strict readings should be taken as DZSO is responsible for injuries if wind has exceeded limit and you have given signal to jump.
  3. Assign your personnel to various jobs and be sure there are sufficient drivers ready to take equipment back to airstrip after first two or three jumpers have landed. You remain in center of circle and measure all distances less than 150 ft. Jumpers should be critiqued by DZSO as to their maneuvering and PLF.
  4. No directions should be given to jumper in the air other than those necessary to insure a safe landing.

PERIOD 13

SUBJECT: **Door Exits and Basic Turns.**
TIME .1 Hour.
TRAINING AIDS: Model of Human Figure.
           Charts Showing Door Exits, Body turns.
AREA: Classroom.
  I. Introduction:
    Purpose is to introduce the student to the methods of door exits and turns, holding a heading, and reviewing the basic body positions.
      a. A parachutist should learn to make door exits to enable him to properly depart from various types of aircraft, hold a heading since this is a

competitive requirement, and make turns to insure that he can open over the proper opening point.

    b. Review body positions and the common errors.

    Include buffeting, uncontrolled turns, uncontrolled falls, spins, and barrel rolls, stressing causes.

II. Explanations:

  1. Door Exits:

    a. Needs for immediate stabilization on exit:

      (1) Immediate and continuous ground reference and orientation.

      (2) Stability relaxes jumper which, in turn, gives jumper more confidence in his ability.

      (3) Parachute won't foul with jumper on opening.

      (4) Style is judged almost immediately on exit.

    b. Clear aircraft facing into the direction of flight.

    c. Avoid any body rotational movement. (Be careful of vigor).

    d. Align yourself with flight of aircraft.

    e. The higher the aircraft speed, the deeper the delta position of the arms on leaving aircraft.

    f. On small doors, bend at the knees, not the waist.

    g. Discuss:

      (1) Straight out exits.

      (2) Exits toward tail of aircraft.

    h. Questions and discussion of door exits.

  2. Basic Turns:

    a. Once stable fall has been learned, student may start turns.

    b. First attempts made during free falls of from 10 to 15 seconds delays, after about eight seconds body is close to terminal velocity and settling on cushion of air. In order to guide the turns, student must select a reference point on the ground.

    c. Start with medium delta position. After about eight seconds bring right hand smoothly and steadily over the head, arm curved and parallel to the body. Keep the left arm outstretched with hand at waist level.

    d. Body will then start a turn to the **left**. To accelerate the turn, bend sideways from the waist into the direction of the turn.

    e. To halt the turn, straighten the torso, draw back the right arm and advance the left arm. When the turn has stopped, return both arms to the desired position of fall.

    f. The easiest position from which to turn is the medium delta. In the full delta turns are rapid and the beginner generally over-controls the turn.

    g. Learn to lead your body in turning. There will be a delay of about one second before the turn takes effect. In stopping the turn, counter the turn **before** arriving on the new heading.

    h. For practice, make full 360 degree turns to both the right and left. Based on the speed of the turn, start slow countering actions after about three-quarters of the turn has been completed.

    i. Beware of losing track of time and altitude!

    j. Question and discussion period.

SECTION XIV

CLUB FORMS

In order to accurately determine each club member's pattern of performance, current jump status, capabilities and limitations, past performance and future potential, it is most necessary that written records be kept by each club.

These records should be as few and simple as possible. With the records shown herein, which are few and simple, a club Safety Officer will have a complete history of every jumper in his club, their mistakes, performance, and potential.

All forms are self explanatory. The problem lies in seeing that they're filled out promptly and correctly.

The main form is the Club Membership Record. On this goes the necessary initial background data, followed by the ground training record, and then the static line and delayed fall jump record. This and the Club log should be the permanent verification records of the club.

The grading forms are temporary for any particular jump period and, once the information from these forms have been entered onto the Membership Record and Log, they can be destroyed. The Club Secretary should insure that the main records are posted promptly after each jump period and then make them available to the Safety Officer. It is more important to record each mistake made than the things that the member did well since it's the errors made that concern the Safety Officer.

In addition to the forms shown, an individual packing and maintenance record should be kept for each parachute showing the date and name of the packer (for each repack) and any maintenance performed on the parachute.

CLUB CARD NUMBER:......................

PCA Card Number:...........................

INDIVIDUAL TRAINING/PROGRESSION RECORD

Date Training Commenced:..

Last Name:.., First Name .... MI........, Age........

Address:..M..........
F..........

Name and Address of Next of Kin:...

Number of previous jumps: Military S/L................Other: S/L................F/F:.............................

Previous Parachute Clubs:..

Medical Certificate Date:...............................Parental Waiver Date:..

TRAINING DATA

(Make remarks and notes on reverse side/as numbered.)

First Orientation: Date...........................Instr:............................Note No............................

1st Parachute Familiarization: Date:................Instr:.................................Note No....................

Packing Sessions: 1: Date:....................Instr.............................Note No.....................

2: Date:....................Instr.............................Note No.....................

3: Date:....................Instr.............................Note No.....................

4: Date:....................Instr.............................Note No.....................

Packing Test: Date................Instr:........................Result:.............

Exit Training: Date:...........................Instr:.......................................Note No....................

Stable Fall Positions: Date:..... ....Instr:.............................Note No....................

Parachute Openings and
  Emergency Procedures: Date...................Instr:.......................Note No....................

Canopy Manipulations: Date:.........................Instr:..............................Note No....................

Parachute Landings: 1: Date:............................Instr:.............................Note No....................

2: Date:............................Instr:.............................Note No....................

3: Date:............................Instr:.............................Note No....................

Review: Date:........................Instr:..Note No....................

Performance and written
  Pre-Jump Test: Date:............................Instr:............................Results................

CERTIFIED FOR 1st STATIC LINE JUMP. Date:..Instr................

1st S/Line jump: Date:............Note No...........	1st F/Fall: Date................Note No...........
2d S/Line jump: Date:............Note No...........	2d F/Fall: Date................Note No...........
3d S/Line jump: Date:............Note No...........	3d F/Fall: Date................Note No...........
4th S/Line jump: Date:............Note No...........	4th F/Fall: Date................Note No...........
5th S/Line jump: Date:............Note No...........	5th F/Fall: Date................Note No...........
6th S/Line jump: Date:............Note No...........	6th F/Fall: Date................Note No...........
7th S/Line jump: Date:............Note No...........	7th F/Fall: Date................Note No...........
8th S/Line jump: Date:............Note No...........	8th F/Fall: Date................Note No...........
9th S/Line jump: Date:............Note No...........	9th F/Fall: Date................Note No...........
10th S/Line jump: Date:............Note No...........	10th F/Fall: Date................Note No...........

CERTIFIED FOR FREE FALL:

Date:........................Instr:...

TRAINING NOTES

Reverse side of training record form)

Enter all comments regarding the performance and attitudes of the student. Indicate the note number in the space provided on the front of the sheet and number the corresponding comments below.

Note No.	Comments:

COMPETITION RECORD

Date	Location	Type of Jump	Remarks

DZ EVALUATION FORM

Type Plane:.....................Place.....................Date.....................

Jumper No.	Name	Parachute Maneuvering	Landing Distance	Remarks

....
Signature of DZSO and Grader

(1) Information to be filled out in detail.

(2) In block for parachute maneuvering include ability to judge distance, turn canopy and slip, utilizing prearranged signals from ground.

(3) In block for landing include whether landing was with or against wind; for student jumpers, landings should be into or against wind.

(4) Distance to spot or center of circle should be paced off if less than 150 feet or estimated if more and should be indicated by yards or feet.

REMARKS:

JUMPMASTER EVALUATION FORM

Type Plane:.....................Place:.............................Pilot:...........................

Lift No............Jumpmaster.......................................Date...........................

No.	Name	Type of Jump Planned	Exit	Position On Pull	Remarks

Signature

(1) Under type of jump planned use abbreviations found in logbook, i.e. SD/DRCP, FF, DF.

(2) In block for actual jump, describe the jump briefly utilizing code letters whenever possible, i.e. 2Z3SD5/180RT.

(3) Under exit position describe whether stable or if not what caused unstable position.

(4) Position on pull for free fallers and DRCPs should be described.

(5) Remarks, specific, on back side.

PARACHUTE CLUB JUMP LOG

No.	Name	Date	Place	Plane Type	Flying Time	Pilot/Jumpmaster Signature-Lic. No.	Type Chute	Type Jump	Delay in Sec.	Remarks

SECTION XV
BASIC EQUIPMENT STANDARDS
(PCA SAFETY STANDARDS)

I. EQUIPMENT-PHYSICAL REQUIREMENTS:

A. Purpose:

1. This chapter outlines current Federal Aviation Agency policies and Parachute Club of America requirements for the modification and alteration of the; a) main (non-approved) parachute of a dual parachute pack; b) harness, fittings, and attachments, and c) approved TSO articles and/or military parachutes considered to be approved; to be used in sport parachuting.

2. All the items referred to in paragraph 1, above, are governed in full or in part by Federal Aviation Agency, Federal Aviation Regulations Part 65 and 105, and the following FAA definitions:

a. As indicated under FAR 65.129 and FAR 65.125 (b), (1), a centificated master rigger only, may alter a parachute in a manner authorized by the Administrator or manufacturer.

b. Authorization for altering an "approved" parachute (either a TSO article or a military parachute considered to be "approved" under the provisions of FAR 105.43) must be obtained from the parachute manufacturer (preferably) or the FAA.

(1) If for some reason the approval of the manufacturer cannot be obtained, engineering approval for the design changes involved may be obtained from an FAA regional office. It will be necessary for the modifier to submit drawings and data including, if necessary, tests and analyses to establish that the parachute design as modified continues to comply with the requirements of TSO-C23 or with the applicable MIL design standards in the case of military parachutes.

3. In compliance with paragraphs 1 and 2 above, the following will apply:

a. Main parachute of a dual parachute pack:

(1) Assembly of, shall have been accomplished under the supervision of an FAA Master or Senior Parachute rigger.

(2) All modifications or alterations to the main parachute and its components shall have been performed by or under the supervision of the personnel listed in paragraph 2a above and be stamped accordingly, or in the case of military clubs be approved and stamped accordingly by a qualified military board recognized and appointed by PCA.

b. Deployment device; shall have been manufactured by an individual listed in 2a above, and be stamped and dated accordingly.

c. Harness, fitting and attachments: the "D" ring installation shall have been performed by an individual, as listed in paragraph 2a above, and in addition shall meet the following requirements.

(1) The reserve parachute attachment installation shall be examined for adequacy of stitching, stitches per inch and thread size used. The stitch pattern should not be less than a 4 point cross

stitch through the main lift web capturing a nylon webbing which will withstand a tensile strength test of 5000 lbs., buffer strap looped thru the "D" ring or snap and sandwiched between or behind the plies of the main lift webs. The minimum buffer looped length shall not be less than six (6) inches. Stitching shall not be less than 5 cord nylon or equal, with 5 to 8 stitches per inch. Minimum equipment necessary for attachment installation shall be a sewing machine, Singer Model 97-10 or equal.

      d. The reserve (emergency) parachute:

      (1) Shall not exceed a maximum rate of descent of 25 feet per second, per TSO-C23.

      (2) If altered from original manufactures design said alteration will be accomplished in strict compliance with 2a through b-(1) above.

      (3) The reserve parachute used in sport parachuting shall be plainly marked as follows:

      (a) Without Pilot Chute: "Pilot chute removed. This chute eligible for sport jumping only."

      (b) With Pilot Chute: "This chute eligible for sport jumping only."

SECTION XVI

I'm sorry, Miss LaTour, it was an oversight on my part.

WATER JUMP PROCEDURES

1. QUALIFICATIONS:
  a. Class "C" license or equivalent.
  b. A complete briefing and drill period must be conducted by PCA licensed instructor or Area Safety Officer.
  c. Must be a swimmer and inflate flotation gear prior to or upon entering the water.
  d. ASO Approval, see 5 b.

2. DRILL PERIOD. (Not less than ½ hour).
  a. Each jumper regardless of previous experience, must be instructed in the procedures necessary to remove his parachute equipment prior to engaging the water.
  b. A suspended harness using all personal jump equipment to be used on actual jump, including reserve and tie down, must be used to ensure complete understanding by the jumper of the harness escape techniques.

3. MINIMUM EQUIPMENT:
  a. Helmet
  b. Sneakers
  c. Shorts—T-shirt
  d. Flotation gear:
  1) 3/16" full Wet Suit is considered adequate flotation gear.
  2) Any other Coast Guard approved flotation gear.

e. Reserve parachute, if a tie-down is used, one side must have quick-ejector hardware.

f. Main parachute assembly, if the harness does not have quick ejector hardware, such as the B-12 Air Force assembly, one quick-ejector piece of hardware should be used on the right leg strap. The inclusion of an adjustable quick-ejector snap on this leg strap does not require any major alteration, and may be accomplished by FAA certificated rigger. Merely remove the exiting snap and replace it with an adjustable quick-ejector snap. Any properly certificated rigger may perform this operation.

Minimum Instruments: A water-proof stopwatch is suggested for delays of over 10 seconds when jumping above and into the water. Reason. Depth perception over water is extremely unreliable.

4. PREPARATION:
a. Plan jump in writing.
b. Prepare aircraft for parachuting.
c. Set altimeter (aircraft).
d. Check stopwatch (jumper).
e. Brief pilot.
f. Rehearse water jump procedures.
   1) Getting out of harness.
   2) Inflating flotation gear.
   3) Malfunction and emergency.
   4) Brief boat crew on recovery and control procedure, include special instructions for malfunction and reserve deployment.
5. CONTROL:

a. Clear jump with the ASO, FAA, USCG, local aviation officials, sheriffs department and other local law enforcement agencies. Compliance with FAR Part. 105 (new) is mandatory.

b. Written ASO approval for each participant, no blanket waivers acceptable.

c. No less than one boat per jump aircraft standing by (there should be one boat for each jumper in the aircraft, in the event of extreme spotting errors, etc.).

d. Boat personnel should include one qualified parachutist and no less than one qualified life guard.

e. Jump controlled from boat by prearranged signals by qualified parachutist.

6. Normal wind drift and spotting techniques.

7. AFTER PARACHUTE INFLATION:
   a. Check canopy.
   b. Check drift angle to target area.
   c. Unhook belly-band.
   d. Unhook reserve on one side.
   e. Slide saddle forward, (if possible).
   f. Unhook leg strap (leftside).
   g. Unhook chest strap.
   h. Upon entering water, unhook right side leg strap (quick-ejector side) and leave harness.
   i. First, board boat, then recover equipment.

SPECIAL NOTES: Drilling the prospective water jumper in a suspended harness, regardless of previous experience, is most essential. Without the benefit of this pre-jump training the jumper can be expected to contact water with much, if not all, his gear on.

Use of quick-ejector hardware on the right leg strap of an Air Force or any harness without quick-ejector hardware is essential to easy escape from the last leg strap. Many times the harness saddle is difficult to slide forward. To help facilitate moving the saddle forward the adjustment on the diagonal back straps can be left somewhat looser than usual. Should sliding the saddle forward prove fruitless, the jumper can bend his leg and trunk toward each other (on the snap side he wishes to unhook). The slack created by this movement is usually sufficient to allow the snap to be unhooked.

The most important thing to the success of any of the procedure above is drilling the mind and body through practice.

Like I told yuh, Fred, night jumps are just like day jumps.

NIGHT JUMP PROCEDURES

1. **GENERAL:** A night parachute jump is not like the normal day parachute jump, in that there is, 1) an infrequency of such jumps, 2) the possibility of disorientation in delayed fall, 3) the lack of familiar ground reference points, 4) the unreliability of depth perception, 5) the high closing speed, 6) possible euphoric situation and impaired vision, make night jumping a potential danger to the participant which require special consideration for their conduct.

a. Spotting at night offers the jumper an immediately apparent problem; e.g., lack of familiar ground references, general disorientation, and the impaired night vision (above 5,000). At least two sources of information must be relied upon to determine a reasonable flight compass heading, exit and opening point; 1) a topographical map of the DZ and surrounding area, and 2) FAA Flight Service Information to obtain surface and loft wind velocities (wind speed and direction).

1) Topographical orientation must stress location of water, power lines and other specific hazards in the jump area.

2) Night jumps are discouraged in winds exceeding:

(a) Surface—12 m.p.h. (0-1,000')

(b) Loft—18 m.p.h. (1,000'-and up)

b. Disorientation relating to the general feeling of euphoria that may be encountered requires that the jumper be completely briefed, drilled and know exactly what he intends to accomplish during the jump. The psychological differences of a night jump requires that the participant pull his ripcord when in the slightest doubt as to his situation.

(Incidentally, note how much of the above relates to the normal day jump.)

2. QUALIFICATIONS:

a. All requirements of the Safety Regulations are to be complied with, including the posting of NOTAMS with the addition of the following:

1) Participants must be the holder of a valid US FAI Class "C" or higher license or its equivalent.

a. Equivalent experience is: a minimum of 75 stable delayed fall jumps consisting of at least:

    5—stable delays of at least 5" duration
  10—stable delays of at least 10" duration
  10—stable delays of at least 15" duration
  15—stable delays of at least 20" duration
  20—stable delays of at leas 30" duration
  10—stable delays of at least 45" duration
    5—stable delays of at least 60" duration

2) Night jumps may be made only with the written approval of the Area Safety Officer or a valid PCA licensed Instructor. Clearance will be given by name, and the altitude specified for each participant, no blanket clearance may be issued.

3) Participant must have completed within 60 days previous to the intended night jump, a complete briefing and drill period to be recorded in the participant's individual log book by the instructor. Entry to read, "Certified qualified for Night parachute jumping," date and signature of recording official.

4) Night relative work is discouraged and if conducted shall comply with the following:

a. No more than two (2) parachutists may participate in night relative work jumps. Waiver of this requirement may be made by the PCA Area Safety Officers or Instructors.

b. Night relative work jumps may not be conducted from an altitude of less than 7,000 feet above the DZ.

c. Break-off altitude will be 4000' above the DZ Maximum horizontal displacement between jumpers will be accomplished after break-off; maneuvers to be only those necessary to establish maximum horizontal displacement between jumpers.

d) Staggered openings are required, generally:

1st man at 2500 feet
2nd man at 2800 feet
3rd man at 3100 feet

In addition to the normal jump gear, the following additions apply:

3. EQUIPMENT:

a. Lighted instrument panel. (Insure that bulb is covered to prevent glare.)

b. Flashlight—to check canopy and ground.

c. A light visible for three (3) miles in compliance with FAR Part 105, paragraph 105.33.

d. Clear goggles only permitted, if worn.

e. Altimeter and stopwatch, or altimeter only on all jumps of over five (5) seconds in duration.

f. Road flares may not be used by parachutist as illumination during free fall.

g. Manned target with manifest (order of jumps), lighting equipment and transportation.

h. Whenever possible, communication between DZ and aircraft should be maintained.

4. DRILL PERIOD:

Each jumper, regardless of previous experience, must participate in the required briefing and drill period as follows:

a. Use of the topographical map and FAA Flight service information together to compute flight compass heading, exit and opening point.

b. Technique of canopy check at night.

c. Reserve activation, use suspended harness and if necessary, a blindfold for instructional purposes.

d. Disorientation in delayed fall; and methods of counteracting them:

1) Buffets
2) Spins
3) High closing speed
4) Other possible uncontrolled fall positions.
5) When in doubt PULL.

5. JUMPMASTER PROCEDURE:

In addition to the normal Jumpmaster duties as outlined in the SR's the following pre-jump checks apply:

a. Prior to boarding aircraft:

(1) Instrument check—Aircraft and jumpers altimeter at zero.

(2) All individual lighting equipment functioning.

(3) Review of aircraft safety procedures:

(a) Seat belts on to 1,000 feet

(b) Minimum movement in aircraft; protect reserve ripcord handle.

(4) Review of target lighting procedure, compass heading approach.

b. Pre-exit check:

Recheck personal altimeter against the aircraft altimeter and the instrument lighting system prior to aircraft exit and a. (4) above.

6. TARGET CONFIGURATION:

The following target configuration is easily adaptable to most any DZ situation. Participants should not decrease the number of lights used. It is strongly suggested that an orientation flight be conducted and the area explained by the senior jumpmaster or pilot, familiar with night landmarks of the DZ area with each group of jumpers preceding the actual jump run. Other points to consider are:

a. Suggested minimum physical equipment for target:

1) Eight (8) number 10 cans using kerosene and paper or a com-

parable number of 15 to 20 minute road flares (total number depending upon number of intended jumps).

2) Fire prevention equipment: fire extinguishers, shovels and sufficient personnel.

3) No less than a four (4) man ground crew.

4) Ground to air communication, (whenever possible).

5) Target, optional, but should be used.

b. Target triangle to be governed by paragraph 1, a. 1 and the following:

1) Over 18 mph or higher surface wind: all DZ lights to be extinguished, no jump situation.

2) DZ target lights should be placed about 30 paces (approx. 100′) from center of target in triangular pattern. As surface wind shifts occur two (2) additional cans may be used to mark the surface wind line change as well as jumper's opening point. Surface wind line markers should be placed at about 5 pace intervals from each other, depending upon the jump altitude above DZ.

Figure No. 1—Basic configuration indicating any angle approach, exit and opening point.

Figure No. 2—Additional lighting used to indicate direction of flight and parachutist's approximate opening point.

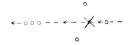

Figure No. 3—Use of 3 directional markers, to indicate direction of flight, surface winds in excess of 12 m.p.h., and parachutist's approximate opening point.

Wrong spot or not, Fred, you've got to learn to relax in competition!

THE CONDUCT OF MEETS

Sport parachuting would not be a sport without competition. Arranging these meets requires a good deal of work and organization. Therefore to make the task easier for those concerned, the following planning guidance on the conduct of parachute meets is presented for your use.

Experience has shown that most meets fall down due to a lack of prior preparation and incomplete planning. There is an old cliche that says that if you take care of the little problems, you'll never have any large ones. In the case of parachute meets, it is felt that this is particularly applicable.

Let's start off by saying that parachute meets should be as inexpensive as possible for everyone, and the sponsoring club shouldn't try to pay off the mortgage from the event.

Further, let's divide a meet into seven phases:
1. Preplanning.
2. Invitation, Publicity and Replies.
3. Arrival of Contestants.
4. Conduct of the Meet.
5. Concluding the Meet.
6. Departure of Contestants.
7. Post-meet actions. (Sounds like D-Day, doesn't it)

PRE-PLANNING

Once a club has decided that it will host a meet, a planning committee (meaning: let Fred do it, it's his idea) should grab the meet by the tail (phew!) and nail down the answers to the following problems.

a. **Events**

Planning for events should be based on the capabilities of the jumpers expected to attend the meet. If they are novices, use simple events and even include static line events. If they will be mixed, include events for novices, and events for advanced jumpers. If they are to be highly skilled, include national or international type events. A recommendation is always to include an accuracy event and a style event and base the complexity of the event on the capabilities of those expected to attend. Since the host club is responsible to make up the events, it will have to decide how simple or complex the events are to be.

b. **Qualifications:**

This ties in with how complex the events are to be. The host can restrict entry by specifying certain license qualifications or it can open the meet to all comers. If the events are too simple, advanced jumpers won't come and if they are too difficult, the novices won't compete. The licensing system of PCA has been designed so that jumpers can be placed into catagories to insure qualification for various levels of competition. Thus certain events can be organized for Class B jumpers, others for Class C, etc. These qualifications should be set as the events are planned. If PCA licenses will not be required, it is recommended that the statement, "equivalent of a Class ....License" be used for clarification.

It is recommended that all competitors be PCA members as part of their qualifications. This insures that each jumper is covered by PCA insurance which lessens the burden of the host club from future damage or spectator injury claims. (It also supports the PCA from whom you may receive assistance in planning your meet . . . another of the many services brought about through membership dues.)

Be certain in establishing qualifications to state that jumpers are not permitted to enter an event for which they are not qualified.

c. **Equipment Restrictions:**

The host should prescribe any restrictions relative to equipment to be used. This concerns specific canopy modifications, canopy porosity, palm releases, automatic openers, etc. Most important is the fact that a qualified rigger should be appointed to examine each contestant's equipment prior to the meet to insure that it is airworthy and that the reserve is sealed and in date. A time and place should be allowed for this activity and the main parachutes should be broken into and examined. Critical points to be especially watchful for are ripcord housing, tacking, pins, cones, and Capewell assemblies, reserve D-ring installation, correct pilot-chute and sleeve assembly, and functioning instruments.

Operational Equipment:

(List of minimum equipment needed at the end of chapter.)

d. **Number of Clubs to Be Invited:**

Of course, this depends on the facilities available to feed and billet the contestants plus having enough aircraft and jumping facilities and personnel to conduct the event properly. Remembering that the major reason to get together in a competitive meet is friendly competition and fun, strain should not be placed on the contestants to find economical housing and food.

e. **Date and Time of Meet:**

Dates should coincide with favorable weather periods. Hosts should insure that no major public event is being conducted during jump periods which would pull the public away from the jump events—particularly when the host is depending on a paid admission to support the meet financially.

Jumping should commence as early as possible after daylight due to the favorable weather conditions at this time.

Experience has proven that a three-day week-end is the best time for a meet, however, the meet should be terminated early Sunday afternoon to allow tired contestants an adequate amount of time to drive home safely. Remember, the most dangerous period in parachuting is the drive to and from the airport!

A written time schedule should be prepared and given each participant on arrival. This schedule should commence from the night preceding the meet until its conclusion. One of the greatest faults of most meets is that the participants don't know the schedule of events or where to go for different activities. This can be eliminated easily with a written schedule and controllers to guide everyone necessary. This also applies to the attending public. A mimeographed flier for the public is cheap and saves many headaches.

f. **Airport and Aircraft Support:**

The ideal solution for a jump meet is to have the jumping done on the airport being used. Care must be taken to insure that jump traffic does not interfere with aircraft traffic—including transient aircraft with radios—and vice-versa.

Proper clearances must be obtained in advance for the use of the airport from airport, city, county, state, and federal authorities. Runways closed during the meet must be properly marked.

The loading zone should have a sketch or air photo (for designating hazards, escape areas, etc., and for marking wind-drift indicator location) of the drop zone available to the jumpers and pilots. The aircraft climbing area, descending area, and general jump pattern should be drawn on a sketch and available to the pilots prior to each run. The pattern will vary according to wind conditions so the chart must be used to brief pilots and jumpers with each change. A sample pattern is as follows:

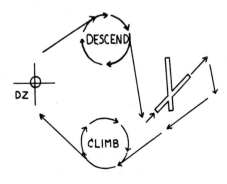

All aircraft used for competition must maintain radio contact with a ground control operated specifically by meet personnel at the drop zone. Each pilot must be cleared from ground control prior to commencing the jump runs. Since events differ in altitude, each event should be completed prior to commencing another event at a different altitude. In a style event, the pilot can be used to radio the number of the jumper, after exit, to the judges below.

Aircraft used for competition should be capable of carrying three or more jumpers and have a fast rate of climb to prevent unnecessary delays between jumps. On this basis a lift of three jumpers will take an average of twenty minutes. Of course, when more aircraft are available, more jumps can be made in a shorter amount of time. It is recommended that no more than four jumps be made in any one day and that three jumps per day per contestant is ideal.

Pilots used for competition should have previous experience in dropping parachutists. When this is not possible, endeavor to allow inexperienced pilots to drop some fun jumpers prior to a competition flight.

Aircraft must be properly certified for door and seat removal.

g. **Drop Zone Organization:**

The success of a meet depends on the smooth flow of contestants from the packing area to the manifest area to the standby area to the loading zone to the drop zone and return to the packing area. If the DZ is not at the airport the problems of control and timing are multiplied.

The key to controlling the entire operation is an adequate public address system, particularly at the packing-loading area. It is also necessary to have a reliable person in charge of each area, even though they may be close together. It is recommended the following general set-up be used:

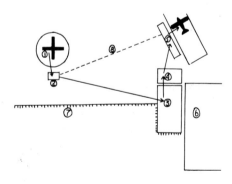

1—Target
2—Chief Judge
3—Packing Area
4—Standby Area
5—Loading Area
6—Contestant Parking
7—Public Viewing Area
8—Radio/telephone Direct communication

Direct communication must be maintained between the DZ and the loading zone, both for control of jumping and posting the master score board or sheets. The scoreboard is highly important since it keeps all jumpers informed of their standing at all times.

The packing area should be placed close to the public observing area since it creates a great deal of interest. However, it should be roped or fenced off so that only contestants are permitted inside. Mats should be provided at the rate of about 1 mat per twelve contestants. The packing area should be as clean and smooth as possible.

The manifest area should have a table and chair for the manifester plus communication with the DZ. The manifester should also control the loud speaker to announce flight orders and control the loading. This loudspeaker should be focused on the standby area.

h. Procurement of Judges:

The best and most impartial judges available should be used for any competition. If none are available locally, the organizers should write for outside judges. An attempt should be made to subsidize the judges' travel, food, and housing expenses during the competition. We suggest no less than three judges per meet: a chief judge, an accuracy judge, and a style judge.

i. Procurement of Awards and Trophies:

The only advice which can be given here is to endeavor to obtain them as economically as possible according to your budget. Better yet, endeavor to get them donated by local merchants.

j. Written Rules:

The rules of the meet should be written well in advance as to the system of scoring and loss of points. The major thought to remember is to keep all rules as simple as possible. The major objective is to determine and grade proficiency.

k. Agencies which Might Sponsor a Meet:

Kiwanis, Lions, Chamber of Commerce, Jr. Chamber of Commerce, Knights of Columbus, VFW, American Legion, various businesses, schools, etc. Let's face it, a parachute meet is good business and good publicity in any area!

l. Billeting and Feeding Accommodations:

Should be as near as possible to meet area of operations. An endeavor should be made to acquire some decent, cheap—or free—billets (School gyms, Legion halls, etc.) or at least some clean, indoor area where bunks and mattresses could be furnished for the jumpers to lay out a sleeping bag. And don't forget the lady members . . . as if we could!

m. Transportation:

Determine availability of local transportation for DZ and to and from billet area, if necessary.

INVITATIONS:

After the above points have been resolved, invitations should be sent out to the clubs concerned. The invitation should be sent at least 45 days prior to the meet and contain the maximum information for a club to use in planning for its entry. Don't forget, the more detailed advance info you can make available to them, the better their chances of participating—and the more the merrier.

The following information in an invitation should give any club a pretty good picture of what the meet will be like:

a. Date and times of meet. Alternate date if weathered out.

b. Events of contest.

c. Qualifications of entrants.

d. Equipment restrictions, if any.

e. List of clubs invited (separate list).

f. Rules of meet and scoring procedure.

g. Altitude and location of DZ.

h. Location of billets.

i. An estimated cost (minimum for meet) to include: Entry fees, billets, meals, transportation, etc. If the area is an expensive area, this should be noted.

j. Transportation to jump area, if necessary.

k. Place of reporting on arrival and persons to be contacted.

The more advance notice a club gets, the more opportunity it will have to get in some local publicity about the forthcoming event, which will be good for parachuting in the big picture. The fact that a local club is competing in a state or national meet is good local club publicity and eventually will arouse people to ask how the club did and, subsequently, will build interest in the local jump group. The ultimate aim is to get sport parachuting onto the sport pages!

REPLIES:

All clubs should make an extra effort to be prompt in replying to an invitation received and this will also make the work of the sponsoring club much easier. If a club is not going to participate, a post card to this effect is all that is necessary and takes only a minute to write. Clubs accepting the invitation should send along the names, jump qualifications, and experience of their contestants so that the sponsor can use this information for pre-meet publicity.

ARRIVAL:

The sponsoring club should arrange for a central point to which contestants will report, somewhere near a transportation center. Registration can also be accomplished at this time and then guides and transportation can take the arrivals to their billets. Rules for the meet and administrative intructions can also be handed out at this point.

MEET:

Prior to the meet a meeting should be held by the judges, pilots, and contestants to clarify any questions about the meet. Rulings on malfunctions, excessive wind gusts, traffic patterns, order of jumping, body maneuver judging, etc., can be ironed out during this period.

MEET PERSONNEL:

Judges: a. Not less than three for each event.

b. For style events, each Judge should be furnished one timer and one recorder to assist him.

c. For target accuracy one should be the chief judge, one the accuracy measurement judge, and one the timing judge. The timing judge should have one recorder assistant. The measurement judge should have 3 markers (fichets).

Loading Zone: 1 Master-of-ceremonies-type PA announcer.

1 Manifester.

1 Shuttle vehicle driver.

1 Air-ground communicator.

111

Packing Area: 1 Rigger-Equipment Safety Officer.

Standby Area: Master Scoresheet Clerk (also Meet Clerk) Contestant Coordinator.

OVERALL:

It is desirable to assign one person to coordinate details from the beginning planning to meet completion. This, of course, depends on the dependability of the host club members. The Meet Director should be the coordinator, directing the overall planning and operation. The following groupings should be delegated and coordinated:

    a. Billeting, feeding, transportation

    b. Communication, including PA system

    c. Equipment procurement

    d. Administration

        Clerks

        Guides

        Drivers

    e. Operations:

        Pilots

        Judges

        Asst. Judges

        Recorders

        Commo Operators

        Scorers

        Air-Ground Communicator

FORMS:

The following forms may be used as a guide in producing the necessary records to document the competition:

    a. Hold harmless waiver for each contestant to sign.

    b. Roster of Contestants (Name, competition number, club, age, total number of free falls, FAI license.)

    c. Manifest and loading forms

    d. Accuracy Judging Forms

    e. Style Judging Forms

    f. Master Score Sheet

Once the meet has commenced, a running record of the standings should be posted promptly on a blackboard so that teams and jumpers know where they stand at all times. The board should show, briefly, the jump experience of each contestant so all will know the talent of their competitors.

A specific time and place should be set for sometime during the meet when all club presidents can get together for an hour or more to talk over and compare notes on the operation of clubs, organization and equipment recommendations for the area, parachuting safety procedures and methods, future contests and activities planned, and problems encountered; in other words, an exchange of ideas. This meeting should be held away from the jump area, at lunch-time for example, to insure that it would be short, constructive, and without interruptions.

CONCLUSION:

Plans should be made to present the winners' trophies immediately following the last jump measurement in order to allow participants to get an early start homeward. Most of us work, and, based on past meets, come to the meet in automobiles, which means a long drive home. If a dinner is to be held, it should be on the night prior to the last day of the meet.

After the meet the sponsoring club should send a summary of the event, to include the results, to the PCA.

MEET EQUIPMENT LIST

Judges:
  1 Pair 7 x 50 Binoculars (minimum power)
  1 Stop Watch (1/10 second)
  1 Clipboard and Pencil
  1 Judges identification armband
  1 Ground pad
   Judging forms

Judging Equipment:
  1 Target
  1 Tape measure, 50 feet, steel
  6 Marking pins, steel, with 8" x 1" ribbon (fichets)
  1 Scoring table and chair
  1 Telephone or radio
  1 Blinker signal and ground arrow
   (for ground-signalled style event)
  1 Wind line signal (smoke, sock, arrow, etc.)

Loading Zone:
  1 Table and chair
  1 Telephone or radio
  1 Public address microphone
  1 Clipboard and pencil (carbon paper)
   Manifest forms
  1 Vehicle to shuttle contestants
  1 Air-ground radio

Packing Area:
  1 Packing set per 12 contestants comprised of:
    2 stakes
    1 tension board
    1 apex fastener
    2 shot bags
    1 line separator
    1 packing mat, 3' x 40'
    1 Public address speaker
     adequate fencing
    1 Table and chair, Equipment Safety Officer-Rigger
    1 Clipboard and pencil

Standby Area:
   Benches or bleachers for standby jumpers
   Public address speaker
   Parking area for contestants' autos
   Master Scoreboard, table and chair

1 Clipboard and pencil
1 Footlocker for completed judging forms, blank forms, adminis-
  ministartion forms, etc. This area should be the DZ meet head-
  quarters.

JUMPER IDENTIFICATION					
DATE			TIME OF JUMPERS EXIT		
LIFT NO.	JUMPER NO.	NAME		LEG NO.	
JUDGE			RECORDER		

EXECUTION OF FIGURE					
1st Turn	2nd Turn	Back Loop	3rd Turn	4th Turn	Back Loop

COMMENT: _____

Disorderly Fall @ 200 pts. _____	Overshoots @ 35 pts. _____
Undershoots @ 35 points _____	Overshoots @ 200 pts. _____
Undershoots @ 200 pts. _____	Off-heading (prior to or after the execution of the figure @ 10 pts. per second).

TIME OF FIGURE OR PENALTIES	
Time Figure Ended: _____	Began Figure _____ seconds late @ 35 pts.
Time Figure Began _____	Opened Prcht _____ seconds late @ 1 pt. per 1/10th sec.
Time of Figure _____	
Seconds of Bonus: _____	

SCORING DATA BLOCK	
Total Score Possible (Less Bonus Points)	_____
____ Secs of Bonus pts. @ 5 pts. per 10th second	_____
SUB TOTAL	_____
Less:	
Time Penalties _____	
Style Penalties _____	
TOTAL PENALTIES _____	_____
TOTAL POINTS GAINED	_____

SECTION XIX

MILITARY AND SPORT PARACHUTING

A Comparison

U.S. Army Photo

How many times has a sport parachutist found himself explaining to an interested bystander that the techniques and the equipment used in sport parachuting are quite different from those used by the Airborne Soldier? The same old questions are asked again and again, and the answers are what form the basis for this article.

Because of the tremendous amount of publicity that was given to the "Paratrooper" during the war years, there has been a resulting identification between the word **parachuting** and images of hundreds of helmeted combat troops descending in T-10s'. This identification is a definite asset to the morale of our airborne soldiers. And their very existence and abilities are an asset to the tactical capabilities of our Armed Forces. However, this identification of all parachuting with military parachuting is a definite hindrance to the general understanding of sport parachuting and for that reason it is, in a way, detrimental to the growth of the sport. Our purpose, then is not to detract from the stature of the military parchutist. It is rather to inform the public of the differences between the techniques, equipment and physical quaifications required by military and sport parachuting.

During the second great war, it was necessary to create and train a tough parachute corps. In order to get the breed of men necessary to volunteer for such duty, the missions, deeds and abilities of this group were glamorized. Their qualifications were widely publicized. It was a tough job for tough men and they did a brilliant job. They even shaded the Marines, which was probably tougher than holding Bastogne, which they did also.

Photo Courtesy of PCA

By the end of World War II, the general public had conceded

that military parachutists were tough. The public knew that they went through hard training and conditioning in order to jump, and they accepted the idea that anyone who jumped from an airplane had to be a sort of superman. Now, while this is true for the Army paratroops, the Marine Recon Units, the Navy para-scuba outfits and the Air Force recovery groups, it does not apply to the sport parachutist. It is our job, therefore, to explain to the public that there is about as much similarity between sport parachuting and military parachuting as there is between Sunday motorboating and the Battle of Midway; though similar devices were used, there is simply no comparison.

Some of the obvious differences between military and sport jumping are those which arise as a result of the difference in equipment and jump procedure. In military parachuting, jumpers exit the aircraft on a specific mission and once this mission is set into motion there is no opportunity for cancellation regardless of wind or ground conditions. Sport parachutists have the capability to abort the jump if everything is not properly set such as altitudes, winds or timing. When wind exceeds safe minimums during sport parachuting jumps, jumping is stopped. In the military, when tactical necessity requires the jump, everybody jumps.

Fast air speed exits from military planes make correct opening positions difficult. Slow air speed exits from light planes enhance the capability of even a novice jumper to consistently obtain stable openings.

Military harnesses are bulky and difficult to adjust. The pack requires from 80 to 160 pounds of opening pressure. Sport parachuting harnesses have better individual fitting adjustments, padded fasteners, quick release snaps and Capewill canopy releases. Opening pressure for the sport pack is only twenty-two pounds at the most.

Since military jumpers need equipment on the ground in order to function as a fighting unit, they carry from 50 to 150 pounds of additional gear on a jump. The only additional equipment carried in sport parachuting is an altimeter-stop watch assembly which adds only two or three pounds of additional weight.

Paratroopers jump from 1200 feet in training; sometimes lower in combat. Should a malfunction occur, they have less time to make corrections than does the sport jumper opening at 2500 feet.

The possibility of collision with other jumpers in the air is almost nil in sport parachuting when compared to the salvo of hundreds of jumpers and equipment during mass military drops.

Finally, the experienced jumper engages in controlled free fall which enables him to guide himself to a correct opening point. Free fall is the heart of sport parachuting and its techniques and its pleasures are outside the realm of mass military jumping. After free fall is concluded or even after a sport static-line jump, all sport parachutists employ steerable canopies which again is a source of control denied the military jumper.

These are some of the basic differences between military and sport jumping. It is obvious that both types of jumping are conducted according to the needs and requirements of a sport in comparison to a military unit. One would no more expect an average sport jumper of being capable of the physical exertion required to make a military jump than he would expect the average military jumper to be able to make a thirty second delay.

There is one aspect of military jumping which all sport jumpers could and should think about. That is the safety record of military jumpers. While the military deems that military parachuting is dangerous enough to merit hazardous pay, they have such excellent and rigid training and jumping standards that their accident, injury and fatality rates are amazingly low. A few years ago a test was conducted whereby a parachute division and a ground infantry division conducted training over a given span of time under the same circumstances. The only exception was that the airborne division also conducted training jumps during the same period. The results revealed that the airborne division had less training accidents and injuries, **including** parachuting, than did the ground division! They found that the high degree of safety consciousness which was instilled into the parachutists carried over into all their other duties. The point here is that the discipline and rigid safety regulations required by the airborne offer a good example to the sport parachutist. If this discipline and safety consciousness cannot be enforced by a controlling body in civilian situation, it can be forced on the individual by himself.

The military parachuting safety record was not gained by accident. They did it with dedicated men and discipline. And they made this type of jumping as safe as is humanly possible. If we are going to make sport parachuting relatively as safe, we must also engender this dedication and discipline. There is no substitute.

The next time the father of some would-be young parachutist approaches you on the drop zone and says, "Say, I was in the Paratroops in World War Two and by-golly I'm not gonna let young John here . . .," you can say, "Well, sir, there are certain very important differences between military and sport . . ."

PICTORIAL
The Phases of Sport Parachuting

Packing Parachutes

Exit

Going Up

Free Fall

Spotting

Relative Work

All photos courtesy of Parachute Club of America, U.S. Army,
Tennessee Sky Divers, Jim Pol

Under Canopy

Landing

Final Goal
World Parachuting Champion

1962 Womens World Champion
Muriel Simbro
USA

1962 Mens World Champion
Henry (Jim) Arender
USA

JOIN

the

PARACHUTE CLUB OF AMERICA

P. O. Box 409

Monterey, California

Good Jumping